SECOND EDITION

BLENDED
COACHING

MAJOR NEW REVISION

SECOND EDITION

BLENDED COACHING

Supporting the Development and Supervision of School Leaders

GARY BLOOM • JACKIE OWENS WILSON

CORWIN

For information:

Corwin
A SAGE Company
2455 Teller Road
Thousand Oaks, California 91320
(800) 233-9936
www.corwin.com

SAGE Publications Ltd.
1 Oliver's Yard
55 City Road
London EC1Y 1SP
United Kingdom

SAGE Publications India Pvt. Ltd.
Unit No 323-333, Third Floor, F-Block
International Trade Tower Nehru Place
New Delhi 110 019
India

SAGE Publications Asia-Pacific Pte. Ltd.
18 Cross Street #10-10/11/12
China Square Central
Singapore 048423

Vice President and Editorial Director:
 Monica Eckman
Program Director and Publisher:
 Dan Alpert
Senior Content Development Editor:
 Lucas Schleicher
Content Development Editor:
 Mia Rodriguez
Editorial Assistant: Natalie Delpino
Production Editor: Vijayakumar
Copy Editor: Christobel Colleen
 Hopman
Typesetter: TNQ Technologies
Proofreader: Benny Willy Stephen
Indexer: TNQ Technologies
Cover Designer: Gail Buschman
Marketing Manager: Melissa Duclos

Printed in the United States of America

Library of Congress Cataloging-in-Publication Data

Names: Bloom, Gary, author. | Wilson, Jackie Owens, author.

Title: Blended coaching : supporting the development and supervision of school leaders / Gary Bloom, Jackie Owens Wilson.

Description: Second edition. | Thousand Oaks, California : Corwin, [2023] | Previous edition: 2005. | Includes bibliographical references and index.

Identifiers: LCCN 2023017031 | ISBN 9781071870785 (paperback : acid-free paper) | ISBN 9781071870754 (adobe pdf) | ISBN 9781071870778 (epub) | ISBN 9781071870761 (epub)

Subjects: LCSH: School principals—Handbooks, manuals, etc. | Educational leadership—Study and teaching—Handbooks, manuals, etc. | School management and organization—Handbooks, manuals, etc.

Classification: LCC LB2831.93 .B56 2023 | DDC 371.2/012—dc23/eng/20230502

LC record available at https://lccn.loc.gov/2023017031

This book is printed on acid-free paper.

23 24 25 26 27 10 9 8 7 6 5 4 3 2 1

Contents

Note From the Publisher: The authors have provided video and web content throughout the book that is available to you through QR (quick response) codes. To read a QR code, you must have a smartphone or tablet with a camera. We recommend that you download a QR code reader app that is made specifically for your phone or tablet brand.

List of Figures and Tables

FIGURES

TABLES

Foreword

It has been about 18 years since the original publication of *Blended Coaching: Skills and Strategies to Support Principal Development*. Since that time, over 35,000 copies have been sold and *Blended Coaching* continues to be an essential text for those engaged in training and supporting educational leaders.

Many of the challenges that we faced in K-12 education 18 years ago remain in place today. We continue to struggle to close the achievement gap that mirrors and reinforces the inequities in our society. Simply put, we fail far too many of our students. We continue to face a daunting shortage of candidates for teaching and leadership jobs in our schools. We struggle with high turnover fueled by the demands of the job and the difficult working conditions encountered by professional educators. The political polarization that is fracturing our communities is being manifest at district and classroom levels.

On the other hand, there is reason to be optimistic about the future of K-12 education. More than ever, teachers are being recognized as professionals and are being asked to serve as leaders in their professional learning communities. The impact that principals have upon student achievement has been well documented, and districts across the country have developed career ladders that lead from the classroom to the principalship and beyond. Despite the forces that would divide our communities, a commitment to equitable outcomes is reflected in most educational policy and in our new generation of school leadership. And the social-emotional dimensions of teaching, leadership, and learning are now openly discussed.

Along with these hopeful trends has come a recognition of the value of mentoring and coaching support for novice and veteran educators in improving retention and performance. National standards for teacher and principal supervisors now call for coaching, and novice teachers and principals are supported by mentoring programs in many if not most school districts.

Mentoring- and coaching-based support were not the norm when Gary Bloom, Janet Gless, Wendy Baron, and I founded the New Teacher Center at the University of California Santa Cruz in 1998. The NTC's work, grounded in the work of the Santa Cruz New Teacher Project, quickly grew to become a national model that produced well-documented positive impacts on teacher retention and student achievement. Early on in our work it became clear that teacher effectiveness was directly influenced by site leadership, and that school principals would benefit from the same sort of support we were providing to teachers. Our principal coaching work was soon adopted in many states and districts around the nation.

It became clear that the strongest schools and districts were ones where coaching and mentoring were embedded in the culture at all levels and at all career stages. Among other things, we were the first organization to write about the importance of principal supervision and to provide training for principal supervisors grounded in coaching.

It was this work which resulted in the development of the leadership coaching model that is described in Blended Coaching. The Blended Coaching model and book explicitly addressed conditions that we encountered in the field; that being an effective leader demanded both technical knowledge and skill, and "ways of being".... Dispositions and interpersonal skills. These "ways of being" often went unaddressed in preservice programs and other professional development models.

In the years since the original publication of *Blended Coaching*, Gary has continued to develop the concepts articulated in *Blended Coaching* in collaboration with colleagues including coauthor Jackie Wilson.

In the first edition of *Blended Coaching*, we state that "coaching is not supervision… but effective supervisors coach, a lot." In this new edition, the authors explicitly support the practice of coaching-based supervision, an approach to supervision that is focused upon growing those being supervised rather than merely rating them.

The authors have also broadened the focus of the book to address the value of coaching for educators in many roles in addition to the principalship. They have also updated the book to reflect current professional standards, while refining tools for the development of basic coaching skills.

Eighteen years ago, in the original edition, we brought attention to the importance of developing educators with the commitment and skills to address issues of equity in our schools. Wilson and Bloom renew that focus in this edition.

With the publication of this updated edition, it is my hope that a new generation of educators will continue to recognize and develop the power to change the world for the better through collaboration, coaching, and community.

—**Ellen Moir,** Founder and Former Executive Director,
New Teacher Center

Preface

Welcome to *Blended Coaching: Supporting the Development and Supervision of School Leaders.*

The first edition of this book was entitled *Blended Coaching: Skills and Strategies to Support Principal Development.* The Blended Coaching model has been widely adopted as an approach to supporting the professional development of educators with many job titles and at all stages of their careers.

In this second edition of *Blended Coaching*, we have broadened the scope of much of our text to reflect the applicability of our approach to teachers, school leaders, and others in the K-12 community. While the bulk of our discussion speaks to the principalship, we suggest that what we share here has much broader utility. We also explicitly address the value of Blended Coaching as the foundation of effective professional supervision.

Schools need teachers, principals, and other leaders who are able to build communities of practice that will enable all students to succeed. These professional educators have a keen ability to promote collegiality, support student and adult learning, and nurture teachers. They encourage all members of the school community—students, teachers, and parents—to do their best.

Principals are responsible for setting the tone at their schools. And yet, as is frequently the case with teachers, principals are typically given the keys to the building, a pat on the back, and expected to go forth and succeed. New principals often have little or no supervised work experience and only limited practical preparation. Veteran principals struggle with changing expectations and increasing demands. Teachers practice in relative isolation, often receiving little or no actionable feedback. As the current generation of principals and teachers retires, school districts must contend with a well-documented shortage of candidates who have been suitably prepared to assume leadership and teaching positions.

Recognizing the importance of quality site professional development, school districts and other institutions around the country are currently working to establish more effective models of support for new and veteran educators and pipelines to insure a supply of quality candidates. Calls for such programs have been issued by many national and state organizations. Professional organizations that represent school leaders such as the American Association of School Leaders (AASA), the National Association for Secondary School Principals (NASSP), the National Association for Elementary School Principals (NAESP), and the Council for Chief State School Officers (CCSSO) have been advocating for high-quality preparation programs to better prepare aspiring school leaders who will eventually take on the role and responsibilities of Assistant Principal, Principal, and Superintendent. Professional organizations such as the University Council for School Administration and the International Council of Professors of Educational Leadership that represent faculty who teach in preparation programs have been engaged in discussions about program quality and support. Organizations such as Learning Forward, Center for Educational Leadership at the University of Washington, the Leadership Academy, and the National Policy Board for Educational Administration have been working to establish more effective models of support for new and veteran educators and pipelines to insure a supply of quality candidates. Philanthropic organizations such as the Wallace and Joyce Foundations have provided financial support for innovative approaches to developing principal pipelines.

This book offers a fresh approach to professional development and supervision for principals and other educators. *Blended Coaching* addresses several critical needs:

- The importance of sustained, stable, and effective site leadership for school improvement

- The increasingly severe shortage of qualified candidates for the principalship and teaching positions

- The inadequacy of traditional preservice and inservice programs

- The need for quality induction and professional development programs for educators that include a mentoring or coaching component

- The need for effective coaching based supervision for principals, teachers, and all support staff in the education community.

This book is about helping principals and other school leaders bring themselves and their schools to their highest potential—by clarifying and then achieving their goals. It is about teaching, showing, guiding, and working side by side with school leaders to help them improve their performance. We believe the subject we address is of interest to all who are concerned with school improvement, including supervisors and faculty in administration preservice programs, central office personnel seeking to improve the quality of site leadership, and individuals now serving as coaches or mentors to school leaders around the country, as well as those charged with formal supervision.

Norma is the brand new principal of Río Dulce Elementary School. She's 32 years old and grew up in the community where she now works. She was a successful teacher for five years and served as a middle-school assistant principal for eight months before being tapped for the principalship at Río Dulce. She is bright, motivated, and very knowledgeable about teaching and learning. Two weeks into the school year, however, she finds herself struggling with an array of issues that threaten to overwhelm her.

The purpose of this book is to help you help principals like Norma meet the challenges they face, survive the rough spots, and thrive in the important work they do. By supporting Norma in her work, you help her make a difference for the teachers, staff, students, and families of Río Dulce School.

Perhaps you are another principal in Norma's district and you have been asked to serve as Norma's mentor. Perhaps you are Norma's supervisor and are only a few years out of the principalship yourself. You might be a retiree brought in by the district to assist new principals, or an independent consultant hired to provide leadership training. You might be Norma, unsure about how to proceed with the supervision of a veteran teaching staff. In all of these scenarios, Blended Coaching and Coaching-Based Supervision are likely to be helpful tools.

Rose is in her second year as principal of Elm School. The staff appreciates her knowledge of instruction and her support. Although she is highly regarded by her school community and recognized for her commitment and hard work, she describes herself as "burnt out." She is losing confidence in her ability as a principal and is frustrated by the long hours she devotes to her job and her school's slow progress. She fantasizes about quitting. Instead of giving up, however, she shares her frustrations with Raul, her coach, who has built a trusting relationship with her. Raul observes Rose interacting with staff in a variety of contexts and helps her become aware of the ways in which her desire to control and her misgivings about delegating responsibility have burdened her and disempowered others. Raul helps Rose develop new structures for delegation and set personal limits on the number of hours she will work and the responsibilities she will take on. As a result, Rose becomes more comfortable stating her expectations and supervising her staff. By the end of her second year, she feels as if she has emerged from a bad dream—the kind where you are unable to outrun the monster that's close on your heels. Her job as principal becomes manageable, her attitude turns positive, and she begins to look forward to her third year at Elm.

It is our hope that this book will bring you to a new understanding of the concept of coaching and how it applies to the care and nurturing of school professional educators like Norma and Rose. Skilled coaching has helped both Norma and Rose to emerge as outstanding instructional leaders who have had a significant positive impact upon their students. It is our aim to help individuals and organizations to design and implement programs that provide the intensive, individualized, and focused professional development so sorely needed by educators like Norma and Rose.

Coaches, no matter what their particular approach, must apply a variety of basic *skills*. These include building trust, listening, observing, questioning, and giving feedback. Coaches must also learn a number of *strategies*, the fundamental game plans that underlie coaching practice. We have developed *Blended Coaching Strategies* as a model for their application. Coaches should also come to the table with *tools*, those practical resources that shape the coaching relationship and from which a coach can draw to provide feedback and meet the coachee's specific job-related needs. Each of these elements—skills, strategies, and tools—is addressed in this book.

Coaching is a complex art, and expert coaches typically bring years of informal mentoring and other experience to the process. Many coaches have training in a variety of communication and adult learning models, including peer and cognitive coaching. Even if you have this kind of rich background, we hope you will think of this book as an introduction to the profession of leadership coaching. We believe it is essential that you broaden your capability by participating in interactive training and by being part of an ongoing community of practice where you can continue to develop your coaching expertise in the company of like-minded colleagues. Coaching requires practice. Just as teachers improve over time as they plan lessons, deliver the instruction, and assess the learning of their students, the same is true for effective coaching. One does not show up for a coaching session with no plan. Effective coaching requires thoughtful planning in order to target the time spent with the coachee on the greatest need for improvement and growth.

If we are to construct school leadership development programs that attend to the needs of adult learners through coaching and mentoring approaches, it is necessary to establish a coaching model that can be taught, implemented, and evaluated. The goal of this book is to share our model with you and to lay the groundwork for the creation of professional communities where coaching support and coaching-based supervision lead to powerful learning and efficacy for both staff and students.

Acknowledgments

We would like to acknowledge Claire Castagna, Ellen Moir, and Betsy Warren, coauthors of the first edition of *Blended Coaching*. Their conceptual and written contributions are woven in throughout this new edition.

The New Teacher Center at the University of California Santa Cruz and the Delaware Academy for School Leadership at the University of Delaware served as incubators for this work. The Stupski and Wallace Foundations provided critical financial support. School districts and colleagues around the country have contributed to this work through their collaboration and feedback.

Jill Baker and her team in the Long Beach Unified School District have generously shared their time and talent with us. The Long Beach Unified School District has implemented the sort of vision we share here with passion and commitment.

Michael Saylor, Director of Educator Excellence, at the Delaware Department of Education and the Leadership Specialists from the Delaware Academy for School Leadership in the College of Education and Human Development at the University of Delaware who prioritize blended coaching for school leaders as essential to their induction and professional learning and shared the data on coaching trends to inform our work.

Nicole Cathey of the Leadership Academy provided us with valuable suggestions as we worked on this new edition.

We thank Hilary Mead at the University of Delaware for reading, editing, and providing us thoughtful and knowledgeable guidance regarding the relevance of content, resources, and readability of this book.

About the Authors

Gary Bloom is the lead author of *Blended Coaching: Supporting the Development and Supervision of School Leaders*. Gary has 40 years of K-12 education experience, having served as a bilingual teacher, principal, director of curriculum, and assistant superintendent. He served as the superintendent of the Aromas-San Juan Unified School District, known for its innovative programs, such as graduation exhibitions, a teacher-led high school, and teacher peer review. More recently he served as superintendent of Santa Cruz City Schools. He was a founder and Associate Director of the New Teacher Center at the University of California Santa Cruz. Gary is a Kellogg National Fellow, was adjunct faculty to San Jose State University's Educational Administration graduate program, and has consulted, trained, and presented on a variety of topics throughout the United States and in Latin America. He is the primary author of a number of professional development programs for leadership coaches and school principals. He has published articles in a variety of journals, most recently on the topics of teacher leadership, principal development, professional learning communities, new teacher support, and the appropriate use of technology. He authored, with his friend Marty Krovetz, the book *Powerful Partnerships*, a guide for the development of assistant principals in collaboration with their supervising principals available from Corwin. Gary currently consults with and trains in school districts around the United States and Central America, and provides executive coaching to superintendents and principal supervisors.

Jackie Owens Wilson has been an educator for 48 years. She has 30 years of experience in PK-12 education including teaching, literacy specialist, assistant principal and principal for the Indian River School District in Delaware. She was named Delaware's National Distinguished Elementary School Principal (NAESP 2002) and a USDOE National Blue Ribbon School Principal (2001). She served as the Director of Professional Accountability at the Delaware Department of Education, responsible for licensure and certification, quality of preparation programs for teachers and school leaders, professional development, and school leadership. After retiring from the public school system, Jackie served as Program Coordinator for Southern Delaware at Wilmington University for several years. Dr. Wilson is currently an assistant professor in the School of Education at the University of Education where she teaches and advises graduate students in the EDD and MED programs. She has served as the Director of the Delaware Academy for School Leadership (DASL), a professional development, research and policy center in the College of Education and Human Development at the University from 2010 to 2022. In 2015–2017, she led the merger of three professional development centers and designed a comprehensive model of professional development that includes content and leadership coaching and professional learning for teachers and principals. In her role at DASL, Dr. Wilson led a team of leadership specialists providing professional development and coaching support to education leaders in Delaware and school districts across the United States. Notable accomplishments include the development and funding of the Delaware's Governor's Institute for School Leadership; the design and approval of an alternative route state approved principal preparation program; serving as the lead consultant to NASSP for their School Leaders Academy focused on using design thinking for school improvement; and creating a principal pipeline model for school leaders that includes ASPIRE for teacher leaders, STEP-UP for Assistant Principals, and Design Thinking for Advanced Principals. Dr. Wilson is the Executive Director of the National Policy Board for Educational Leadership. NPBEA is a national alliance of major membership organizations committed to the advancement of school and school-system leadership. Member organizations represent the educational administration profession and collaborate to improve the preparation and practice of educational leaders at all levels. She co-chaired the national standards redesign committee that developed the Professional Standards for School Leadership and has been engaged nationally in the redesign of principal preparation programs aligned to the PSEL/NELP standards.

PART I

Coaching Basics

In Part I, we explore the foundations of coaching as a tool for the professional development of school leaders and other educators. We define coaching, and we tie the power of coaching to what we know about how adults learn. We examine the uniquely challenging role of the principal and touch on the complex set of knowledge and skills that principals must possess. We pay particular attention to emotional intelligence and cultural proficiency as prerequisites to success as a school leader. We make a case for coaching as an effective approach for helping school leaders and other educators to develop these competencies.

All coaches, whether coaching fly fishermen, CEOs, or synchronized swimmers, use a set of universal basic skills, such as trust building, listening, observing, questioning, and giving feedback. We explore these foundational coaching skills in the balance of Part I.

An important note: Where coaching is most effective, it is embedded in the organizational culture. Individuals in roles up and down the system are offered coaching support, and coaching-based supervision, as discussed later in this volume, is practiced across the board. That is why, as we have revised *Blended Coaching* to reflect changes in our profession and things we have learned along the way, we are expanding much of the discussion to apply to coaching of teachers and of other professionals in addition to principals. Please note that while we might primarily make reference to principals and other school leaders in much of this text, the approaches we advocate are applicable to the support and supervision of virtually any professional in any role in the K–12 system.

1

CHAPTER 1

What Is Coaching?

oaching is one of those words that is commonly understood but only vaguely defined. The *Oxford English Dic-
tionary* devotes more than a page to the word coach,
first used in the 15th century to describe a four-wheeled
covered wagon used by royalty. In the 17th century, the
word morphed from a noun describing a carriage into one
denoting "a private tutor who prepares a candidate for an
examination."

---

*A coach is someone who (1) sees what others may not see through
the high quality of his or her attention or listening, (2) is in the
position to step back (or invite participants to step back) from the
situation so that they have enough distance from it to get some
perspective, (3) helps people see the difference between their
intentions and their thinking or actions, and (4) helps people cut
through patterns of illusion and self-deception caused by defensive
thinking and behavior.*

—*Robert Hargrove, author of* Masterful Coaching

Today we coach teams, players, our kids, and our employees.
There are birth coaches, executive coaches, and life coaches.
In fact, tens of thousands of groups and individuals offer
coaching services. Hundreds of organizations will train you to
be a coach, and dozens more will certify you once you're
trained. You can find many titles related to coaching at your
local bookstore, including *Coaching and Mentoring for Dummies*
(Brounstein, 2000). There are probably as many variations of
what gets called coaching as there are flavors of music that get
called the blues. There are basketball coaches who specialize
in exploiting players and throwing chairs, life coaches who
promise business and sexual fulfillment, and corporate

coaches who work with executives and bill in four figures per hour. At its best and at its core, coaching is a fundamental practice, something that virtually all of us experience from the time we are infants. For the purpose of this book, we'll define coaching as *the practice of one individual helping another individual or group to develop the internal capacity to clarify, set, and successfully pursue goals.* At the heart of the definition is the notion that a coach helps an individual or group to develop internal capacity. I hire a coach to help me to improve my golf swing, not to swing the club for me. Another key concept is the notion that coaching is goal driven, and that the goals have to be owned by the coachee.

The coach's main role deals with expanding the ability to see contexts, rather than supplying content. The person being coached then sees new ways to utilize existing skills.

—Julio Olalla, coach and trainer

The most effective way to forge a winning team is to call on the players' need to connect with something larger than themselves.... I've discovered that when you free players to use all their resources—mental, physical, and spiritual—an interesting shift in awareness occurs. When players practice what is known as mindfulness—simply paying attention to what's actually happening—not only do they play better and win more, they also become more attuned with each other.

—Phil Jackson, basketball coach and author of Sacred Hoops

Start measuring your work by the optimism and self-sufficiency you leave behind.

—Peter Block, author of Flawless Consulting

A coach is someone who tells you what you don't want to hear so that you can see what you don't want to see so that you can be what you've always wanted to be.

—Tom Landry, football coach

What coaching does is to expand the space of possibilities that someone is—an expansion that requires an external intervention (coaching) to take place. Coaching allows the coachee to observe oneself as a self, to acknowledge the narrowness and limitations of that self, and to expand that self beyond its boundaries, beyond the horizon of possibilities available to the coachee's own intervention.

—Rafael Echeverría, *author of* The Art of Ontological Coaching

If you want to go fast, go alone. If you want to go far, go together.

—African proverb of unknown origin

From Olympic gold medals to NCAA championships, Duke University Men's Basketball Head Coach Mike Krzyzewski is one of the most successful coaches of all time. He attributes his success as a coach to four key concepts, which include:

1. **Create shared ownership**: *Truly successful teams share a sense of ownership. Belonging means more than simply being on the roster. Each member of the team must be emotionally invested in the same goal and must understand what being part of a team means at its core.*

   As a coach you must help the coachee come to the realization that they share ownership of the work in a school with others, and if they are going to lead others they must create shared ownership of the work.

2. **Tailor coaching to the person**: *Adaptability and sensitivity are critical to leadership. The way to coach each person depends on their personality and the situation they are in. Effective leaders think about each individual and tailor their coaching approach. It is up to the coach to use coaching strategies to help the principal or teacher to figure out what steps need to be taken next.*

   An effective coach listens, observes, and adapts his coaching strategies based on the needs of the individual coachee. This flexibility and the ability to demonstrate empathy are very important in building the trust that is necessary to help the coachee solve a particular problem and take a calculated risk.

3. **Unite big egos**: *As a coach you may find yourself working with an individual who has a big ego. Rather than curbing that confidence, the coach has to learn how to use it productively and will succeed by recognizing the individual's passion and redirecting it so it focuses on the instructional success of teachers and the achievement of students.*

An example is the high school principal who is very popular in the community because of the winning football team. He knows everyone in the community because he was the high school quarterback in the school where he now serves as the principal. He is confident and arrogant and does not believe that he needs a leadership coach. He does not understand that the coach's role is to focus on instructional leadership and not football. The coach has to remind the principal to use his talents so it is a collective win for the school and not an individual win for himself.

4. **Show your emotions**: *Coaching and leadership require more than creating an image of strength. Being a strong leader requires connecting on an emotional level. This often depends on the coachee, the context of the conversation, and whether the school is improving or is in decline. There are times when the coach has to show that being vulnerable and emotional is a different definition of strength.*

Deirdra is a principal of an elementary school that serves a population of high needs students. She rules the school with a law and order style that she believes is necessary to manage student behavior. She is very concerned to show any emotion or to get too close to students or staff because she knows this has been the downfall of previous principals. She has tried to be consistent with policies and procedures, holding everyone to the same standard of performance and students to the same standard of behavior. She has been firm with parents and consistent with her communication. Deirdra's coach, Ann, is concerned that she does not appear empathetic to the concerns of teachers. One day when Ann arrives at the school, she finds Deirdre locked in her office and unwilling to meet with her. After some persuasion she enters the principal's office and finds Deirdra in tears. Deirdra confronts her with the following words: "*I lost a student this morning who was hit by a car as he was walking to school. I do not know how to address the staff about this situation without appearing emotional and weak. What should I do?*" Ann walked across the room and with tears in her eyes, said to Deirdra, "*showing love, caring, and sadness are not signs of weakness. You are demonstrating that you are human and that you care for your students, teachers and community. Your demonstration of care and compassion are also signs of great strength.*" Following the conversation, Ann and Deirdra developed a plan to communicate with teachers, parents, and the community before taking a walk through each classroom to console teachers, students, and support staff.

GARY'S REFLECTIONS ON THE FLIGHT INSTRUCTOR AS "COACH"

I learned to fly airplanes a few years ago. In many ways, this was the toughest learning challenge I have ever taken on. The learning process had many dimensions. There were the cognitive challenges of learning a new set of theories, rules, and procedures. There were the physical challenges of mastering a new set of motor and perceptual skills. There were the emotional challenges of overcoming the stress and fear I often experienced while at the controls of a small plane.

The cognitive aspects of flying were easy for me to learn and were mostly self-taught. To get a pilot's license, you have to master airspace regulations, navigation, weather, and many other things, some vital, some trivial. In order to prepare for the Federal Aviation Administration written examination, I studied a text, listened to audiotapes, and practiced with test preparation software. I scored 98% on the written exam. As proud I was of this score, I was far short of being a pilot.

The real work of learning to fly takes place in the company of a Certified Flight Instructor (CFI). This is a one-on-one relationship. From the first lesson, the student sits in the pilot's seat, the CFI alongside. A CFI draws upon a variety of strategies. Typically, new maneuvers are explained by the CFI, sometimes demonstrated, and then attempted by the student with the CFI ever ready to intervene. The CFI draws the student's attention to the indicators, the data sources that measure successful completion of the maneuver. For example, in completing a steep turn, a pilot is expected to maintain a bank angle of approximately 45°, not gain or lose altitude, and roll out of the 360° turn flying in the same direction as when the turn was started. The first time a student makes a steep turn, the CFI talks the student through the maneuver, telling him when to pull or push on the yoke and when to roll out of the turn. After a few rounds of "guided practice," a student should know the effects of his inputs and should be able to identify, on his own, the reasons for an unwanted altitude gain or a failure to maintain heading. Establish trust, demonstrate competence, observe the student pilot, and provide feedback—this is the work of a CFI.

But it is not this simple. Flying is a high-stakes business; small mistakes can lead to fatal consequences. When a CFI certifies that a student is ready to take the practical flight test, he or she is attesting to that student's capacity to take friends and family safely aloft, alone, into the wild blue yonder in a flimsy assembly of aluminum and steel.

When I had a panic attack early in my flight instruction and wanted to get on the ground immediately, my flight instructor complied. He also insisted, after a bitter cup of hours-old coffee, that we go up again. He asked that I relax while he ran through a series of stalls, killed the engine, and brought the plane down to a safe and quiet landing.

When I forgot to retract the plane's flaps at takeoff, resulting in a dangerously sluggish performance, he did not say a thing. When I turned to him and asked if something might be wrong, he suggested that I look at the plane's controls. I never attempted to take off again without checking the flap lever.

When, in my CFI's judgment, I was ready to fly solo, he stepped out of the plane and sent me off, linked to him only by a scratchy radio. When I was ready to fly my first cross-country flight, he reviewed my planning and released me for the trip. He was at the other end of the phone when I called to announce that I had made it back alive.

My experience learning to fly has shaped the way I think about adult coaching. Here are some of the characteristics of the CFI's role and practice that also apply to professional coaching:

- The CFI's job is goal-oriented: to prepare pilots to meet a set of well-articulated performance standards.

- The CFI works one-on-one with students, designing lessons and activities around individual needs.

- At times, the CFI provides direct instruction, explaining, demonstrating, and walking students through maneuvers.

- At times, the CFI observes while a student completes maneuvers independently, for the purpose of gathering data and providing feedback and to assess and build the student's capacity to complete maneuvers without a CFI alongside.

- A CFI seeks assurance that a new pilot is able to make high-stakes decisions and can respond to unexpected events safely and independently. To this end, CFIs use both simulations and the observation of performance in real situations as coaching and assessment tools.

- CFIs attend not only to skill but also to perception and emotion. They teach pilots which instruments and feelings to trust, and which to ignore. They help pilots learn to "fly the plane," ignoring distraction and emotion. They attend to the stress and fear that often accompany flight instruction.

I don't know which is more high stakes or unforgiving: flying a small plane, teaching a room full of adolescents algebra, or leading a school. I know that in all three cases, the support of a CFI—or a coach—can make the difference between going places or "crashing and burning."

OUR DEFINITION OF COACHING

Coaching has been embraced by the private sector because it is a proven strategy for increasing the productivity and effectiveness of managers and executive leaders. As a means of providing deliberate support to clarify and achieve goals, coaching is also well suited to the needs of adult learners in the public sector. In *Why Can't We Get It Right?: Professional Development in Our Schools*, Marsha Speck and Caroll Knipe (2001) outline a number of research findings regarding adult learning that help to explain the success of coaching:

Adults will commit to learning when they believe that the objectives are realistic and important for their personal and professional needs. They need to see that what they learn through professional development is applicable to their day-to-day activities and problems.

Adults want to be the origin of their own learning and should therefore have some control over the what, who, how, why, when, and where of their learning.

Adults need direct, concrete experiences for applying what they have learned to their work.

Adult learners do not automatically transfer learning into daily practice. Coaching and other kinds of follow-up support are needed so that the learning is sustained.

Adults need feedback on the results of their efforts.

Adult learners come to the learning process with self-direction and a wide range of previous experiences, knowledge, interests, and competencies.
—(p. 109)

Direct, job-embedded coaching on a one-on-one basis responds to each of these characteristics of adult learners, whether they lead classrooms, schools, or private enterprises. Effective coaching incorporates a number of key elements:

The coach constructs a relationship based upon trust and permission. True coaching cannot take place in the absence of a trusting relationship. The coachee must be willing to participate in the process—to learn, to grow, and to change in fundamental ways—and feel safe enough to open up and show vulnerability around the most sensitive issues of professional practice. It is the coach's responsibility to encourage this by working continually to build trust and permission. While these dynamic characteristics of the coaching relationship may fluctuate from one instance to the next, they should deepen and strengthen over time.

The coach serves as a different observer of the coachee and the context. One of the most important assets brought by a coach to the coaching relationship is fresh perspective. A coach provides the coachee with data and feedback about the coachee's behavior and the specific situation that may lead to new ways of acting. A golf pro, for example, may help a client make major improvements by pointing out what seem to be minor distinctions in the way the client holds a club. A leadership coach might use a 360° survey instrument to help a principal recognize that they are perceived as unfair because of the ways in which they interacts with some staff members.

The coach and coachee recognize that problems and needs are valued learning opportunities. It was Michael Fullan who penned the words, "problems are our friends" (1993, p. 21). Every problem presents an opportunity to learn and to grow by recognizing systemic issues that, if addressed, can lead to significant improvements. In the coaching process, problems, and needs are sought out and embraced. This concept is at the heart of most coaching interactions.

The coach must be prepared to apply a variety of coaching skills *as appropriate to the context and needs of the coachee*. Effective coaches must master a number of fundamental skills, including listening, paraphrasing, questioning, and assessing the specific needs and contexts of the coachee.

The coach must be prepared to apply a variety of coaching strategies *as appropriate to the context and needs of the coachee*. Effective coaches often use multiple strategies during the course of any given coaching session. The coach may play a *facilitative* role, guiding the coachee to learning through the use of feedback and reflective questions. At other times, the coach might play an *instructional* role and provide expert information, advice, and resources. We call this approach *Blended Coaching Strategies* and believe its use is the foundation of an effective leadership coaching practice.

The coach is fully present for and committed to the coachee. A coaching relationship is unlike most other human relationships in the degree to which the coach attends to the coachee. Some coaches describe coaching as entering an altered state, a unique place where all of their experience, skill, and awareness is focused upon one other human being. The coaching relationship is all about the coachee and helping the coachee achieve specific goals. If you watch a videotape of a coaching session with the sound turned off, you will have no trouble distinguishing the coach from the coachee. A skilled coach directs all attention to the coachee and listens on multiple levels.

The coach provides emotional support to the coachee. Many positions in education—including those of school leaders—are isolated and emotionally challenging. It is an important role of the coach to provide emotional support, offer encouragement, and help the leader maintain motivation and focus.

The coach maintains a fundamental commitment to organizational goals as agreed to by the coachee, and appropriately pushes the coachee to attain them. Although it results in more positive feelings about oneself and one's position, coaching is not intended merely to make leaders feel good, or help them be popular, or ensure that they survive in their jobs. Coaching instead is directed to the attainment of consensual goals. In the case of school leaders, this means helping them make a positive difference for students. An effective coach always looks beyond and beneath any presenting problem, issue, or need, in order to find opportunities for growth and action that will help the coachee establish goals and make plans to achieve them. The coach also holds the coachee accountable to move forward with those plans.

The coach practices in an ethical manner. Professional ethics are critically important in coaching. Careers often hang in the balance, and high-stakes, rough-and-tumble politics sometimes come into play. Coaches must commit to confidentiality. They must carefully and explicitly negotiate their relationships with their coachees' supervisors. They must also be sensitive to and disclose promptly any personal biases, relationships, and histories that might impact their coaching, and they must comply with their agreements with their coachees and other clients.

MENTOR	COACH
• Informal relationship, often between peers • Often unstructured and driven by the mentee's need of the moment • Volunteers for whom the role is an add-on responsibility • Expected to be nurturing and supportive often unstructured and driven by the mentee's need of the moment • Typically, senior to their mentees	• A formal relationship between a client and an individual trained in the coaching role • Is built around a standards-based structure and accountability • Coaches are dedicated to and compensated for their role • Bold in providing feedback and in challenging their clients to improve their performance in ways that push comfort levels • Qualify for the role because of their expertise and may or may not be senior

WHAT COACHING *ISN'T*

In order to clarify the concept of coaching, it's useful to consider what coaching is *not*, and to review some of the practices that are sometimes confused with it.

Coaching is not training. Coaching addresses the needs of the individual rather than conveying a particular curriculum. While coaching can and often does support training activities, training is top–down and centered on content. Coaching, by contrast, is centered on context and designed to respond to the needs of the individual learner.

Coaching is not mentoring, although effective mentors use coaching skills and strategies. The terms *coach* and *mentor* are sometimes used interchangeably. For the purposes of our work, however, we define a mentor as an organizational insider who is a senior expert and supports a novice. A coach is typically from outside the organization and is not necessarily senior—in age or depth of related professional experience—to the coachee. In our experience, novice principals benefit from having both a mentor *and* a coach. A mentor might be that veteran principal across town whom a novice can call to find out what procedures to follow to get her building painted, or how to work productively with the union representative, or whether she really needs to attend the upcoming meeting at the district office. Mentors can show newcomers the ropes in a number of situations. A coach, on the other hand, provides continuing support that is safe and confidential and has as its goal the nurturing of significant personal, professional, and institutional growth through a process that unfolds over time. A coach brings an outside perspective and has no stake in the status quo in an organization. Coaching is a professional practice; mentoring is typically voluntary and informal.

Coaching is not supervision, but effective supervisors coach a lot. There are distinct differences between the roles of coach and supervisor. A supervisor has the authority to give direction; a coach does not. A supervisor has an explicit role in determining a subordinate's employment status; a coach does not. A supervisor may be obliged to report on an individual's progress and problems to a superintendent or school board, while a coach can assure a coachee of confidentiality. A supervisor may have influence over the context an individual works in and the resources available to that individual; a coach does not. However, effective supervisors use coaching skills and strategies most of the time with their supervisees (and therefore have something to gain by applying the strategies and skills outlined in this book) and understand that most of the time their role is the same as that of a coach: to nurture growth in their subordinates. We discuss Coaching-Based Supervision in Chapter 12.

Coaching is not therapy. An effective coach uses many of the same skills and strategies used by therapists. However, therapy focuses on the individual's psychological function, while coaching focuses on the accomplishment of professional goals. Therapy involves understanding an individual's past; coaching helps the individual change an organization's future. Therapy often treats issues of individual dysfunction or pathology; coaching occurs within the boundaries of normal professional issues. It is important that coaches be aware of these boundaries; while they do not aspire to the role of therapist, coaches should be prepared to suggest that coachees seek additional help if personal situations warrant.

SO YOU WANT A COACH?

- Type "coaching for educators" into a Google search and you will get 50,000,000 results.

- EducatorsCoach.com offers to "increase your satisfaction in every aspect of your life" and to help you to "attract more of what you want both personally and professionally."

- While there are multiple businesses and organizations that train and "certify" coaches, the world of coaching can best be described as the Wild West ... anyone can hang a shingle and claim to be a coach.

- Our favorite is a local coach who advertises that she will help you to get out of debt, attract your love partner, and sell your real estate faster (all for a modest fee...).

COACHING FOR PROFESSIONAL EDUCATORS

School leaders and other educators are typically accomplished adult learners who are goal-oriented and have very diverse needs. They are often pedagogical experts and tend to resent and reject poorly designed and delivered professional development. However, they are likely to embrace effective coaching.

In our work around the country, we have asked hundreds of principals, teachers, and others how they acquired the many skills and the broad knowledge essential to their jobs: in the teaching role, in preservice, and in service programs, through life experience, or on the job? They report that their most important learning takes place on the job—and note that preservice programs are among the *least* significant sources of preparation for the principalship.

In a recent report (May 2022) funded by the Wallace Foundation, researchers were asked to find evidence regarding high-quality principal learning. In the report, "the researchers synthesized peer-reviewed scholarship from 2000 to 2021 that addresses principal preparation and development programs and examined survey results and statewide policies. Through this review, key findings, research implications, and policy implications related to principal preparation and training emerge." There were four key findings in the report:

1. High-quality principal preparation and professional development programs are associated with positive principal, teacher, and student outcomes, ranging from principals' feelings of preparedness and their engagement in more effective practices to stronger teacher retention and improved student achievement.

2. An emerging focus on equity-oriented leadership has the potential to develop aspiring principals' knowledge and skills to meet the needs of diverse learners.

3. Principals' access to high-quality learning opportunities varies across states and by school poverty level, reflecting differences in state policies.

4. Policies that support high-quality principal learning programs can make a difference. In states and districts that have overhauled standards and have used them to inform preparation, clinically rich learning opportunities, and assessment, evidence suggests that the quality of principal learning has improved. (Darling-Hammond et al., 2022)

Finding one is significant because it makes the association between principal preparation and professional development and preparedness for the job. Preparedness is important since it leads to engaging in practices associated with teacher retention and student achievement.

And current findings from a report provided by the American Association for Teacher Education (AACTE) Teaching in the Time of COVID-19: State Recommendations for Educator Preparation Programs and New Teachers emphasizes the importance of continuous professional learning, mentoring support, and feedback.

Why is this research important? If we want teachers and principals who are well-prepared for their jobs, then quality preparation matters. Programs that are nationally accredited and meet rigorous standards are important. But even when the educator completes an accredited program, they may still require professional development, mentoring, or coaching support to continue to improve and grow their skills and knowledge.

The education profession is no walk in the park. It can be brutal and lonely work. Principals and teachers often feel vulnerable and insecure. Our research tells us that their outlook and attitudes about their profession run through cycles ranging from desperation to optimism. It is no surprise, then, that educators frequently turn to their coaches and mentors for empathy and reassurance in addition to professional support.

We do not believe that coaches should serve their coachees simply as unquestioning cheerleaders. However, the coaching relationship will be strengthened if the coach communicates confidence in the coachee and if the coach recognizes that an appropriate element of her role is to convey enthusiasm for the coachee, for the coaching process, and for the value of the coachee's work.

Because a successful coaching relationship is based on trust and rapport, coachees must believe in and respect their coaches. When a coach expresses confidence in a coachee, it has a significant impact on the coachee's outlook and performance—an impact that should not be underestimated. Indeed, an important part of the coach's role is to help coachees build and maintain self-confidence and commitment to their jobs. There are times when the most helpful thing a coach can do is lead the coachee through an inventory of the things that are going right and make note of the coachee's strengths. On some occasions, a coach can provide a great service by simply pointing out that the coachee's problems are not unique and offering assurances that they will be overcome. This, of course, is accomplished without a trace of dismissiveness or discounting the nature or seriousness of the problem.

Implicit in the relationship between a coach and coachee is the agreement by which the pair has set goals and in which each party has given certain permissions to the other. We suggest that fairly early in the relationship, as trust and rapport are being built, the coach and coachee have a conversation in which each outlines his or her expectations. Included in the conversation should be considerations such as:

- Developing a shared understanding of coaching
- Clarifying specific goals and focus areas for the coachee's professional growth
- Confirming confidentiality
- Establishing frequency of meetings

- Identifying means of communication

- Affirming commitments to openness

- Outlining activities to be observed and mechanisms for data gathering

- Discussing relationships and communication with supervisors

- Devising mechanisms for reevaluating and revising the relationship

Resource B.1 at the end of this book contains an information sheet titled Making the Most of the Coaching Relationship, developed to provide new coachees with a straightforward explanation of the coaching process. Also included is a sample agreement spelling out basic expectations, to be signed by all parties in a coaching relationship.

CHAPTER 2

Meeting the Challenges of School Leadership

P rincipals are expected to possess educational expertise; to manage large organizations with complex programs, staffing, and budgets; and to work in a politically charged environment with constituencies that include elected officials, bus drivers, recent immigrants, union representatives, parents, novice teachers, business managers, lawyers, and five-year-olds. Principals are expected to be instructional leaders making headway in addressing the many equity issues that pervade our society.

If you're a principal, chances are these scenarios sound familiar.

It's your goal to spend 50% of your time in classrooms, but there are "discipline problems" lined up outside your door, and a concerned parent has shown up and needs to talk with you immediately. Your building union representative wants to meet with you because you have exceeded the number of allowable staff meeting minutes this month in your effort to organize English as a Second Language instruction at your site.

You have received an e-mail from the superintendent asking you to respond to accusations of racial bias in your staffing decisions.

If nothing changes, up to 40% of your students could fail the upcoming high school exit exam and be in danger of not receiving diplomas next spring.

Our leadership coaching work has taught us that principals face a set of common challenges. Each of these can be tied to the professional standards such as the Professional Standards for Educational Leaders (PSEL) set by the National Policy Board for Educational Administration (2015) and each draws upon a broad set of skills, abilities, and knowledge. The professional standards define the nature and the quality of work of persons who practice that profession, in this case educational leaders. They are created for and by the profession to guide professional practice and how practitioners are prepared, hired, developed, supervised, and evaluated. They articulate the scope of work and the values that the profession stands for.

Preservice programs cannot provide adequate preparation in all of the areas that a school leader will need to do their job. They simply cannot prepare candidates adequately for a job as difficult and complex as the principalship, unless they offer long-term preparation that places novices in highly structured internships with master principals for a substantial amount of time. In addition, as demands and expectations change, even experienced principals need support.

PROFESSIONAL KNOWLEDGE AND SKILLS

We can't imagine planning a trip without an itinerary, compass, or GPS to guide us. Even if the trip is to a place we have been many times before, we have learned through experience to expect detours, traffic jams, and car accidents. If we happen to be traveling by air, we can expect delays, cancellations, and unexpected personal disruptions. Even with a plan interruptions may occur. Directions and an itinerary alone are not enough to guarantee a successful journey. Doing some additional preparation in advance is important and often leads to a more enjoyable trip. Reading a travel book or visiting a website in advance of a trip is one way to learn more about the location and its history. Discussing plans with friends who have already spent time in the location provides us with insight about landmarks we may want to see or avoid. The research is necessary to prepare for the journey in order to take advantage of all the opportunities available. We understand the excitement of spontaneity, but skills using a map or GPS and knowledge about tourist traps will prevent me from finding myself in a bad situation. It is better to invest the time in advance in order to make the most of the time we spend enjoying the trip.

So what does planning a trip have to do with the challenges of the principalship? Consider what went into planning for a trip to assure that you have a successful experience for yourself, friends, and family. Moving into an assistant principal or principal position requires planning in order to acquire the skills, knowledge, and expertise to do the job effectively. In our observations and coaching of hundreds of assistant principals and principals, we have seen what can happen when entering the job unprepared.

Throughout this book, we will use short vignettes to provide examples and to help the reader better understand particular situations or problems as we discuss them in the book. Over the years, we have supported many educators who have found themselves facing complex challenges. The storytelling in the book is provided so that you can better understand the situation and the solutions the school leader chose. We will begin with Jake, an assistant principal.

Jake is very hard-working and eager to move from an assistant principal position to the principal role. He fast-tracked his preparation by doing the minimal requirements. He has very little teaching experience and completed certification requirements in an abbreviated program with no internship experience required. He got hired by the district after one interview. because the school needed an assistant principal to take care of discipline.

Jake's district bears some responsibility as he prepares for and enters his new job. If his goal is to become a principal, he needs to prepare as if he was taking a cross-country trip.

Districts often provide aspiring leadership development programs to identify potential assistant principal and principal candidates. The development programs are often designed and facilitated by district personnel in collaboration with an external vendor or university partner. They can provide a variety of learning experiences that contribute to the educators' growth and development, and most importantly, making a decision as to whether being a principal is the best career pathway for them. *Jake should have taken advantage of district programs in preparation to gain skills, knowledge and experiences he will need as a principal. His fast-track approach is like taking the quickest route on a planned vacation. Jake has missed some important stops that would have better prepared him to enjoy his final destination.*

Districts need to establish policies and practices for talent management. Questions that districts should be asking include:

- What are the qualifications we value and need for the person leading our schools?

- Do our job descriptions clearly state the qualifications and expectations of the job responsibilities?

- Do we have partnerships with university preparation programs in order to communicate what we need of graduates in their principal preparation programs?

- What programs have we designed and offered our districts for aspiring school leaders?

- Do we have school leader data tracking systems that we can use for decision-making?

- How are we interviewing potential candidates?

- How do we support them once they are in a leadership role?

Once in a principal role, there is a shared responsibility between district personnel and the individual for gaining knowledge and skills in order to do the job effectively.

Tammy is in her third month as a new Principal at Blue River Elementary School. She had been excited about the new position and feels very confident that she has the experience and knowledge needed to lead the school of 450 students and staff of 45. She participated in the district's aspiring school leaders program, graduated from an accredited preparation program and has three years of experience as an assistant principal at a large elementary school of 1,000 and staff of 100 in another school in the same district. Tammy feels confident in her new role as Principal. She is convinced that she has done everything to gain the skills, knowledge and experience she needs to be an effective principal. Today she will work with a group of teachers to plan intervention strategies for below grade level readers. She has done her own research about quality literacy intervention programs and she met with the district Curriculum and Instruction Director to discuss options. She participated in a webinar led by a national expert on early literacy intervention strategies, and read the book by the authors. She found it so helpful she purchased copies for teachers to read and plans to schedule a book study with them.

Principals are lead learners. They must continue to read, do research, talk with experts, and explore options for improving the experiences for students in their school. Tammy had a great preservice preparation experience, but her learning continues as she is confronted with decisions that require new skills or knowledge. Tammy knows she has to learn more about reading interventions. She also understands that she will need to provide professional development for her teachers on the new literacy intervention program. One road map that Tammy can use to identify effective practices for addressing these challenges is professional standards.

The principalship is a challenging profession that requires professional knowledge and skills. Educators who make the decision to step into the role of leading a school quickly learn that there are expectations from various stakeholder groups about how they should do their job and what they need to prioritize. Entering the position with the expertise necessary to lead the instructional program, create a culture conducive to teaching and learning, and lead change initiatives that lead to greater student achievement for all students is an expectation that teachers, parents, and district personnel have for the principal. The knowledge and skills necessary for effective school leadership are most often acquired by a combination of experiences: (1) prior experience working in schools as an educator; (2) participating in a district or state aspiring school leader program; (3) completing a university or alternative preservice preparation program to gain certification; (4) mentorship and coaching; (5) performance evaluation that includes formative and summative feedback; and (6) research-informed professional development. It is the combination of one or more of these experiences that prepare an educator for the principalship and more specifically to be an instructional leader focused on school improvement.

Principals are expected to be instructional leaders. They do this by observing teachers and providing feedback on the quality of the lesson. Principals provide feedback regarding the lesson objectives and learning goals for students. They provide specific feedback regarding procedures for activating prior knowledge and summarizing the lesson. They determine if the teacher provided a meaningful formative and summative assessment that allows students to scaffold their learning. Yet because a principal was a good teacher does not necessarily mean they have the skills and knowledge to lead others... It is not enough to have been an effective teacher although it helps. Standing in front of a group of teachers, many with more instructional expertise than you and more years in the profession can be daunting. Jackie remembers: "I remember my knees shaking the first time I walked into a classroom to observe a lesson being taught by a teacher with 25 years of experience. I asked myself, '*what can I tell her that she doesn't already know? How can I provide feedback to improve the lesson? How can I make this experience better for students?*' I soon realized I had a lot of good recommendations to improve the lesson because my professional learning journey had provided me with a depth of knowledge and expertise working with struggling readers. I was able to talk with her about assessment strategies, differentiation and grouping, and using rigorous questioning techniques."

Today, we view instructional leadership as an influence process through which leaders identify a direction for the school, motivate staff, and coordinate school and classroom-based strategies aimed at improvements in teaching and learning. The current state-of-the-art concludes that instructional leadership:

- Affects conditions that create positive learning environments for students...

- Creates an academic press and mediates expectations embedded in curriculum standards, structures, and processes...

- Employs improvement strategies that are matched to the changing state of the school over time...

- Supports ongoing professional learning of staff, which, in turn, facilitates efforts of schools to undertake, implement, and sustain change... (Hallinger & Murphy, 2013, p. 7).

The challenges of the principalship have been compounded by the ever-growing demands on schools. Principals are expected to be instructional leaders who create a learning environment conducive to teaching and learning. They must know curriculum, instruction, and assessment while creating a culture of care and support for teachers, support staff, students, and families. Principals must manage people, time, resources, and the demands placed on them by school boards, the superintendent, and parents. The work has become more unmanageable due to the influence of social media, political and racial tensions, and an international pandemic.

Support for principals can no longer be optional. State policy leaders must include funding for induction programs, mentoring and coaching, designated positions for Principal Supervisors, and standards-aligned professional development. Districts must utilize federal, state, and district funding resources to invest in practices that have been found to be effective for improved working conditions for principals. Examples include providing a mentor as part of induction to the district. The mentor is usually an experienced colleague working in the district in a similar role and supportive of the mentee's professional growth. The mentor serves in a support role and provides the assistant principal or principal with knowledge very specific to policies and practices of that particular school district. Training and hiring coaches whose job is to improve the skills and knowledge of the coachee has been found to be an effective strategy for retention and professional growth. Coaching shows considerable promise as a professional development strategy (Bickman, Goldring, DeAndrade, Breda, & Godd, 2012; Grissom & Harrington, 2010; Huff, Preston, & Goldring, 2013). We believe that coaching is the most powerful professional development investment a district can make in growing the skills and knowledge of principals. The professional learning for the principal continues when the district provides a performance evaluation process that includes a process for goal setting, formative and summative feedback, and a personalized professional learning plan.

The growth and development of a school leader continues over time when combined with induction and mentoring, high-quality coaching-based supervision, and standards aligned professional development. The combination of these opportunities provides the principal with knowledge, skills, and strategies necessary to lead the school. If these experiences are all aligned with a set of professional standards, there is cohesion and focus.

STANDARDS AS A ROAD MAP FOR EFFECTIVE SCHOOL LEADERSHIP PRACTICE

Leadership Standards are most commonly adopted or adapted by state departments of education to guide the system for preparing, hiring, and evaluating school and district leaders. Districts develop policies that align to the state approved standards. Many states adopted national standards such as the Professional Standards for Educational Leadership (PSEL) (National Policy Board for Educational Administration, 2015), or they gather a group of stakeholders to adapt the national standards for state or local context. Some states support local control regarding the development and adoption of school leader standards. In these states, school districts create very specific standards based on local stakeholder input. School districts are left with the tasks of operationalizing the standards so that they guide the practices of school and district leaders.

It is important that school leadership standards embody a research and practice-based understanding. Understanding the research literature and best practices for leading school improvement, developing the professional capacity of school personnel, or working with staff to create meaningful engagement of families and the community is essential if the work is to be impactful and sustainable. With this view or mindset, student learning is at the center of school leaders' work. Educational leaders must focus on how they are promoting the learning, achievement, development, and the well-being of each student. The Standards reflect interdependent domains, qualities, and values of leadership work that research and practice suggest are integral to student success. In practice, these domains do not function independently but as an interdependent system that propels each student to academic and personal success. The PSEL are:

1. Mission, Vision, and Core Values
2. Ethics and Professional Norms
3. Equity and Cultural Responsiveness
4. Curriculum, Instruction, and Assessment
5. Community of Care and Support for Students
6. Professional Capacity of School Personnel
7. Professional Community for Teachers and Staff
8. Meaningful Engagement of Families and Community
9. Operations and Management
10. School Improvement

The ten standards are best understood by grouping them into clusters. The first cluster is Curriculum, Instruction and Assessment, and Community of Care and Support for Students. The second cluster is Professional Capacity of School Personnel, Professional Community for Teachers and Staff, Meaningful Engagement of Families and Community, and Operations and Management. The third cluster is Mission, Vision, and Core Values, Ethics and Professional Norms, and Equity and Cultural Responsiveness. The domain of School Improvement affects all of the clusters, which together reflect a theory of how educational leader practice influences student achievement.

Betty is an elementary principal with five years of experience leading West Oak Middle School. The school has 700 students, a 45% poverty rate based on Free and Reduced Meals data, 12% of students have an Individualized Educational Program (IEP), and 10% of the students are classified as English Learners. Betty has been able to recruit and retain experienced teachers. Eighty-five percent of the teachers have a master's degree or graduate course work. Only 5% of the teaching staff have less than three years of experience. The school has an active PTA that is highly engaged in school decision-making. She has been able to hire literacy and math specialists to serve as instructional coaches in classrooms serving Title 1 students. The superintendent has informed Betty that she is being moved to a different school next year because she has been very effective in raising student achievement for all students. Betty's new school is an elementary school with 1,200 students, a 78% poverty rate, 15% of the students receive special education services, and 20% are designated as ELs. The school has a reputation of chronic absenteeism and students with severe discipline problems. Recently the school has seen high teacher turnover resulting in many new teachers with less than three years experience. Betty knows that this new school will be more challenging than her current school. She understands that she will need additional knowledge and skills to tackle her new assignment.

How can Betty use professional standards as a road map or guiding framework to do her job? She knows that she can't just walk in on the first day without a plan. She needs to consider what she needs to know prior to taking over the leadership of the school such as the current student achievement and personnel data, daily schedules, use of curriculum materials, whether an instructional framework is in place, what supplemental resources are available, and what is her budget allocation. As she learns more about the school, Betty will continue to identify strategies she needs to lead the team.

The standards are foundational to all levels of educational leadership. Betty knows that although the school levels differ, the standards are for all levels and all roles of school leadership. She refers to the standards as a starting point as she develops some thoughts regarding a mission and vision for the school. Her core values have not changed just because she will be changing schools. Betty's core values are the guiding principles that direct her behavior and keep her on the right path. She considers them her unwavering guide to the work she does as a school leader. So what might this look like:

Betty reviews Standard 1: Vision, Mission, and Core Values, Standard 2: Ethics and Cultural Norms and Standard and 3: Equity and Cultural Responsiveness. She decides to focus on the following criteria:

Standard 1b: In collaboration with members of the school and the community and using relevant data, develop and promote a vision for the school on the successful learning and development of each child and on instructional and organizational practices that promote such success

Betty will create a leadership team to review relevant data, develop a list of findings, and make recommendations that will be shared with various stakeholder groups for feedback.

Standard 2e: Lead with interpersonal and communication skill, social-emotional insight, and understanding of all students' and staff members' backgrounds and cultures

Betty will host meetings during the summer prior to taking over the school to get acquainted with staff, parents, and students and to begin relationship building.

Standard 3c: Ensure that each student has equitable access to effective teachers, learning opportunities, academic and social support, and other resources necessary for success

Betty will review personnel data, meet with teachers and support staff one-on-one to listen to their concerns and seek answers to her concerns. The standards did not tell Betty how to do her work, but they did provide guidance on the key domains of the work she must focus on to effectively lead the school. The standards serve as the road map that she must travel in order to reach the destination she desires.

As shown in Figure 2.1 (National Policy Board for Educational Administration, 2015, p. 5), the focus of the standards is on student learning. The research, which is the foundation of the standards, shows that students learn when educational leaders create safe, caring, and supportive school learning communities and promote rigorous curricula, instructional, and assessment systems.

Principals must be learning every day. As principals are confronted with problems or challenges, they can look at the problem as an opportunity to collaborate with others to figure out a solution, delegate the problem to someone else to solve, or ignore it. Effective leaders confront the challenges and engage others in helping them find solutions. The standards serve as a guide to problem-solving. Let's return to Betty to look at this more closely:

Betty knows that she must focus on the quality of instruction which includes curriculum materials, instructional pedagogy, and assessment practices as well as teacher effectiveness in utilizing the instructional materials. She also has to create a school culture conducive to teaching and learning. She has to demonstrate to students that she cares about them by providing the support they need to be successful. Turning to the standards to guide her work, Betty identifies the following areas of focus for her work:

FIGURE 2.1 ● Relationship of School Leadership Work to Student Learning

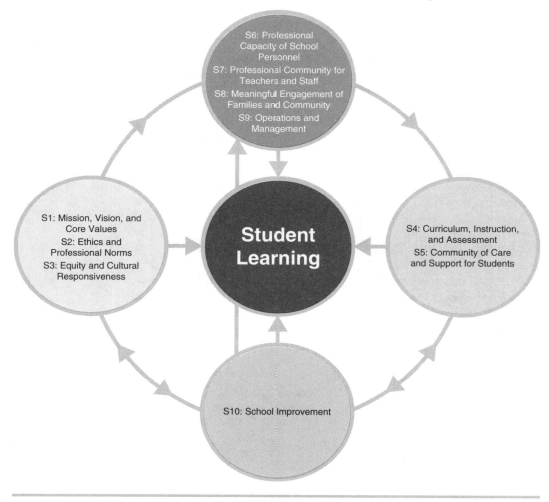

Standard 5E recommends providing coherent systems of academic and social supports, services, extracurricular activities, and accommodations to meet the range of learning needs of each student.

Betty will need to talk with teachers, support staff, and parents to learn more about the current academic and social support programs that are in place at the school and whether they have been successful. She may need to do some research by talking with principals in schools that have similar challenges, reading books of school redesign, and working with external partners who have more expertise in creating a coherent system of support.

As an instructional leader focused on student learning, Betty will need to look at Standard 4, Curriculum, Instruction, and

Assessment to research strategies for promoting a rigorous curriculum, instructional pedagogy, and assessment practices.

Standard 4a states that effective leaders implement coherent systems of curriculum, instruction, and assessment that promote the mission, vision, and core values of the school, embody high expectations for student learning, align with academic standards, and are culturally responsive.

Betty will need to design a plan for determining if a coherent system of curriculum, instruction, and assessment is already in place at her new school. And just because the curriculum has been adopted by district policy does not mean that staff have been provided the professional development they need. Meeting with district office personnel who may be more knowledgeable regarding the curriculum and support available for special education or ELD students will be important steps for Betty to consider.

The work of school improvement and instructional leadership requires educational leaders who can build and strengthen a network of support focused on improving the professional capacity of teachers and staff. The principal must seek out the knowledge required to do the day to day operations of managing a school and also the work of growing and developing the professional community where teachers and students learn and work. They must understand their school community including those who have children attending the school and those who support the school externally. School leaders must have the skills and knowledge about all stakeholder groups in order to develop, communicate, and steward the school's mission, vision, and core values. Educational leaders must act ethically and with professional integrity while leading with an equity-centered mindset and culturally responsive practices. Finally, principals like Betty must believe their school can always be better. These principals are unshakeable change agents who are creative, entrepreneurial, and risk takers who make their schools places where each student thrives.

The PSEL Standards provide the pathway for Betty to improve skills and knowledge to more effectively lead her school.

COACHING ALIGNED TO PROFESSIONAL STANDARDS FOR SCHOOL LEADERSHIP

The goal of coaching is to contribute to the professional growth and development of the principal or coachee. Rather than randomly determining what knowledge a coachee needs, trained coaches assess the skills and knowledge in order to determine a focus by asking specific questions, administering assessments such as Strengths Finder (Rath, 2007), or meeting with the supervisor in advance to determine priorities for coaching. The most important thing is to determine an area of focus for coaching conversations in order to maximize the time on topics with the greatest potential for professional growth. Let's take a look at Dave and Devon. Dave is an experienced school leadership coach. Devon is a principal who is struggling in an area that the superintendent has recognized and is seeking improvement.

Dave has been asked by the Superintendent to coach Devon. Devon has been a principal for two years at a rural school of 450 elementary students and an experienced teaching staff. The former principal retired after leading the school for 15 years. The Superintendent meets with Dave and shares that he has concerns that Devon lacks skills in providing actionable feedback to teachers following a classroom observation. After reading several of Devon's lesson observation write-ups, Dave notices that there seems to be a lack of understanding of the math curriculum. The feedback Devon is providing to teachers attempting to implement the new program is very general and lacks the specificity to improve the quality of their lesson planning and delivery. The Superintendent asks Dave to work with Devon to improve his knowledge of the new math curriculum and his teacher observation feedback skills.

In this example, Dave can look to the PSEL Standards for guidance. Standard 4 focuses on Curriculum, Instruction, and Assessment. The criteria for PSEL Standard 4 provide Dave with specific actions that he can use to focus his coaching sessions. For example, criterion 4c and 4d may be skill deficits for Devon.

Standard 4c: Promote instructional practice that is consistent with knowledge of child learning and development, effective pedagogy, and the needs of each student.

Dave will need to consider if Devon has adequate knowledge about the students in his school. Does he review transcripts of new students, analyze grade distribution for teachers at the same grade level, and talk with specialists about struggling students? Does he attend parent conferences with teachers to listen to parent concerns? These are questions Dave can ask during a coaching session that will lead to a robust conversation between the coach and coachee.

Standard 4d: Ensure instructional practice that is intellectually challenging, authentic to student experiences, recognizes student strengths, and is differentiated and personalized.

During a coaching session, Dave can plan his questions in advance to determine if Devon has the knowledge and skills necessary for this kind of instruction.

Dave has been asked to improve Devon's skills to provide feedback to teachers to improve their instructional effectiveness. To do this, Dave needs to focus on PSEL Standard 6: Professional Capacity of School Personnel. Dave can determine in advance of his coaching sessions which criterion is most appropriate based on his assessment of Devon's skills and knowledge. For example, Dave may decide that his coaching sessions will need to focus on 6c, 6d, and 6e, which include:

6c. *Develop teachers' and staff members' professional knowledge, skills, and practice through differentiated opportunities for learning and growth, guided by understanding of professional and adult learning and development.*

6d. *Foster continuous improvement of individual and collective instructional capacity to achieve outcomes envisioned for each student.*

6e. *Deliver actionable feedback about instruction and other professional practice through valid, research-anchored systems of supervision and evaluation to support the development of teachers' and staff members' knowledge, skills, and practice.*

THE IMPORTANCE OF DATA COLLECTION

Dave needs to identify specific targets for improvement that are relevant to the focus of the superintendent's concerns. This begins with data collection. Developing some baseline data about the coachee is important if you want to measure progress over time. Dave may want to collect the following data in consultation with Devon to identify areas for improvement:

1. Reviewing and analyze recent teacher evaluation feedback documents
2. Determine professional development attended relevant to teacher feedback (curriculum and pedagogy)
3. School resources such as reading or math specialists for support

Once baseline data have been collected, the coach can begin to develop a coaching plan with the principal focused on two to three priority areas. Maintaining records following each coaching session and coding them to the leadership practices identified in the professional standards can provide the coach with important information regarding the needs of the coachee. Dave may want to create a Google document that identifies the targets aligned to the standards and record notes following each coaching session.

One example of how data can be useful to the coach who may be working with several principals, or a district that has a number of leadership coaches supporting assistant principals and principals, is the data collection process done by the Delaware Academy for School Leadership. These reports are used to track frequency and areas of coaching needs by the assistant principal and principal and to identify trends where additional coaching or professional development is needed.

Following a visit with a principal or assistant principal, coaches record anecdotal notes on a Google document and then code the notes to a standard and criterion. Coaches can use the notes to prepare for the next coaching session and determine if there are specific areas of focus that are not being discussed. Is the principal or assistant principal only interested in discussing operations and management (PSEL Standard 9) or the crisis of the day? By maintaining good records and coding them to the standards, the coach can guide the coaching sessions to areas of focus that the coachee may be uncomfortable to discuss such as feedback to teachers regarding cultural responsiveness (PSEL St. 3 Equity and Cultural Responsiveness) or participating in professional learning communities with teachers to review student work (PSEL St. 7 Professional Community for Teachers and Staff). Each coach can review the data for the principals and assistant principals they work with for planning. The data can be disaggregated by coach and coachee.

Why is this information important? One of the goals of coaching is to work with the coachee to strengthen skills and knowledge needed to do the work of a principal or assistant principal. It is important that the coaching visits be focused on strategies that will help the school leader be attentive to the most work using research-informed practices. growth.

Figure 2.2 provides a summary of 123 coaching visits with four coaches working with 23 assistant principals for PSEL Standard 4 Curriculum, Instruction, and Assessment. This tends to be the standard where our coaches spend a lot of time working with principals and assistant principals. The chart shows that the areas of greatest focus for Standard 4 for this quarter are 4c, 4d, and 4e.

FIGURE 2.2 ● Standards Aligned Coaching Data

PSEL STANDARD 4

4C,4D,4E	7	PSEL 4
The substandards that were most frequently seen or worked with during our 123 coaching visits.	The substandards that were observed or worked with eight times or more out of the 123 coaching visits.	PSEL Standard 4 has the highest frequency out of any of the standards worked with in our initial data report and in subsequent data reports.

PSEL Standard 4 Frequency

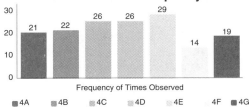

Frequency of Times Observed

■ 4A   ▨ 4B   ▨ 4C   ▨ 4D   ▨ 4E   4F   ■ 4G

The following graph represents the frequency of specific PSEL Standards we have observed and worked with out of 123 total coaching visits.

UNIVERSITY OF DELAWARE.

4c) Promote instructional practice that is consistent with knowledge of child learning anddevelopment, effective pedagogy, and the needs of each student

4d) Ensure instructional practice that is intellectually challenging, authentic to student experiences, recognizes student strengths, and is differentiated and personalized

4e) Promote the effective use of technology in the service of teaching and learning.

If coaches are working with principals and assistant principals to further develop their skills and knowledge as instructional leaders, it makes sense that the coaching conversations would be aligned to Standard 4. Throughout the pandemic when students were receiving virtual instruction, coaches reported an increase in criterion 4e: *Promote the effective use of technology in the service of teaching and learning.*

A second example in Figure 2.3 shows the emphasis on PSEL Standard 6 Professional Capacity of School Personnel. Coaches found they were spending more time on Criterion 6d, 6h, and 6i. The added stress of the pandemic created conditions where coaches were supporting and coaching assistant principals and principals to reflect and develop strategies to address their personal and professional health and well-being, and the work-life balance of the faculty and staff.

FIGURE 2.3 ● Assistant Principals' Coaching Data for PSEL Standard 6 Professional Capacity of School Personnel

PSEL STANDARD 6

6D/6H/6I	7	6B
The substandards that were most frequently seen or worked with during our 123 coaching visits.	The substandards that were observed or worked with eight times or more out of the 123 coaching visits.	These sub-standards were only observed twice out of 123 coaching visits. Once for last data run.

PSEL Standard 6 Frequency

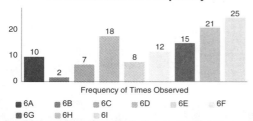

The following graph represents the frequency of specific PSEL Standards we have observed and worked with out of 123 total coaching visits.

Frequency of Times Observed

■ 6A ■ 6B ■ 6C ■ 6D ■ 6E ■ 6F
■ 6G ■ 6H ■ 6I

UNIVERSITY OF DELAWARE

6d) *Foster continuous improvement of individual and collective instructional capacity to achieve outcomes envisioned for each student.*

6h) *Promote the personal and professional health, well-being, and work-life balance of faculty and staff.*

6i) *Tend to their own learning and effectiveness through reflection, study, and improvement, maintaining a healthy work-life balance.*

ISSUES OF EMOTIONAL INTELLIGENCE

The Professional Standards for Educational Leadership provide the evidence-based practices of the work school leaders do in districts and school. But, as important as professional knowledge and skills are, it is no secret that school leaders often fail not because they lack brains, determination, knowledge, or skills but because of what is often characterized as "style" or "people skills." *Emotional Intelligence* (EI) is the term Daniel Goleman associates with this set of elusive competencies and dispositions that don't show up in most preservice programs. Goleman cites his own research and the work of others in arguing that EI has at least as much to do with on the job success as cognitive intelligence and technical expertise. He defines EI as "the capacity for recognizing our own feelings and those of others, for motivating ourselves, and for managing emotions well in ourselves and in our relationships" (Goleman, 1998, p. 317).

Few jobs present as many challenges to an individual's EI as the principalship. An effective principal must confront a broad spectrum of educational and management issues while building and maintaining relationships with multiple constituencies. The principal is expected to lead change processes in highly politicized and conservative institutions. No wonder, then, that most principals who leave their positions do so for reasons more related to EI than to their knowledge of reading programs or their ability to build a master schedule.

While principals are individuals with unique strengths and needs, we have noted some commonly encountered emotional potholes that challenge both beginning and experienced principals. The following scenarios emerge from our work. Each includes an illustration of the role of the coach in working through these issues. Each resonates with what Goleman calls the four components of EI: self-awareness, self-management, social awareness, and relationship management.

Making the Transition From "One of Us" to "One of Them." Most new principals have come up through the teaching ranks in their districts, if not at their own sites. Like it or not, in the culture of most schools, an administrator is no longer regarded by teachers as a colleague. A new principal may feel like the same person she was before donning the administrator hat, but she will be treated differently by friends, former colleagues, and community members. Recognizing and accepting change in how we are perceived can be a difficult adjustment.

Susan is a new principal who finds herself in an awkward situation that many novice principals experience. A coach can be a great support in some of these difficult situations.

Within the first month of her first principalship, Susan was forced to respond to parent complaints about Jean, a friend and former teacher colleague. Jean expected unquestioning support from Susan; the parents were looking to their new principal to respond to their concerns. Susan was perplexed and torn by this situation, one that radically changed her relationship with a colleague of many years. Susan's coach helped her monitor her emotional responses to this situation, analyze Jean's interests and those of the students and parents, and develop an appropriate action plan. Susan's coach also helped her recognize the need to build a new support network where it was safe to share these difficult problems in confidence.

Becoming a Supervisor of Adults. Most new principals have little or no experience as supervisors and evaluators. It is a long emotional leap to become comfortable establishing clear expectations of staff and then following through on them. Tough personnel problems demand that principals manage their own emotions, including anger, empathy, and guilt; deal effectively with the emotional responses of adults; and use the system to serve the best interests of students.

Mike thought the job of principal would be primarily working with students. What he quickly learned that the role of principal is also about working and managing adult behavior.

Mike did not expect to spend dozens of hours during his first months in the principalship dealing with the night custodian. But when rooms weren't being cleaned and the cafeteria wasn't set up for assemblies as requested, he knew he had to step in. His intervention was met with the night custodian's defensiveness and complaints about the lead custodian. Mike's initial reaction to this backlash was to back off for fear of hurting feelings and alarming the union and the district office. With his coach, Mike talked through his emotional reaction to this state of affairs—and as a result, he managed to build a process of accountability for the night custodian that involved the lead custodian, the district maintenance supervisor, and the classified employees union.

Living Under the Spotlight. Principals are surprised by the degree to which their every gesture is subjected to widespread scrutiny. The principalship is a form of celebrity (or notoriety) and requires some surrender of privacy and the freedom to be oneself. Principals must learn a new level of automatic metacognition and impulse control. Every vocalization, decision, and action must be filtered through the questions, "*How will this be interpreted? How will this serve my desired ends?*"

Jack was in a meeting with his coach when two parent volunteers entered his office asking for the key to a closet where supplies for the upcoming Halloween carnival were stored. His response to the two mothers was, "Please, I'm in a meeting. I can't lend you the key now, but I'll be out in a half an hour or so." It didn't take long for the word to get out among parent volunteers that Jack was rude and unappreciative. Jack's coach helped him to develop a less abrupt style of communication, to express appreciation, and to be more attuned to the ways in which people were likely to respond to him.

Letting Go of Emotional Responses to Problems. Principals are assaulted by dozens of problems, large and small, every day. In order to manage their personal stress, they must separate themselves from those problems. And in order to lead their sites effectively, they must set aside their gut responses to problems and approach them instead from a systems perspective.

Carlos was the first Latino principal of a school in transition from serving a largely African American student body to a student population that is primarily Asian and Latino. The previous administrator of the school was African American. It was not unusual for Carlos to be accused of racial bias in his handling of discipline incidents and personnel problems. In this charged environment, Carlos worked with his coach to set aside his anger at being called a racist. He learned to mediate his words and actions and to listen carefully to all parties. Perhaps most important, Carlos began to build inclusive systems and a culturally proficient staff at his site.

Letting Go of Perfectionism and Control. Most people achieve the principalship because they were very competent in their previous positions. They typically come from jobs that were much more contained, in which they could exercise direct, hands-on control. The principalship is more complex. It requires delegation along with acceptance of ambiguity and the lack of strict control. Living with this new tension can be very difficult for some novice administrators.

Elliott describes himself as "anal-retentive." In his first few months on the job, he panicked over all the things that were "not quite right" at his school. There were the staff members who showed up a little bit late, the messy classrooms, the teachers who were not teaching the adopted reading program, the nonexistent budget records, the poor cafeteria supervision...Elliott felt as if each of these issues and more were entirely his responsibility and considered himself obligated to make things right immediately. Because he lacked confidence in the ability of others to do things to his standards, he hesitated to delegate. Elliott's coach helped him to recognize that he could not turn his school around all at once or all by himself. Only by living with imperfection and sharing control could Elliott help his school truly progress. Once Elliott accepted these concepts, he was able to work with his coach to develop plans for delegation of tasks and for sharing leadership responsibilities.

Accepting That the Job Is Never Finished. Related to the need to let go of perfectionism and control is the requirement that administrators understand the principalship as a job with no boundaries—other than those set by the individual principals themselves.

Lucinda could not believe it. She had always worked very hard and never procrastinated. She had been on top of her work and consistently met her own high standards. But now she was in a daze, working from seven in the morning until nine at night on weekdays, and at least one day every weekend. She was held hostage by the paperwork to be reviewed, the meetings to be planned, the journals to be read. Lucinda worked with her coach to prioritize her work, to delegate tasks to others, and to manage her time. One afternoon, she and her coach did nothing but go through her in-box, deciding what could be ignored, what required a personal response, and what could be delegated. Finally, Lucinda articulated a set of promises to herself and to her family: she would be home for dinner four nights a week, and she would work no more than two weekend days each month.

Taking Care of Oneself. Most people who serve as principals are highly dedicated and very altruistic. They have a hard time recognizing, let alone taking care of, their own needs for support—whether those needs are clerical or emotional. To be effective, principals must learn that investing in their own well-being, including interests and relationships outside of school, is important to the well-being of their schools.

Julie was a mess. By her own accounts, she was working 70 hours a week. She was not eating regular meals, had stopped exercising, and was neglecting her husband and teenage daughter. Her coach helped her to recognize that the patterns she had slipped into were not sustainable and supported her to develop more effective management systems. Julie was able to give herself permission to block out quiet time to work at home to catch up on thinking and paperwork, as well as invest time and resources in her own professional development and physical and mental health.

Developing New Relationships With Authority. Many principals enter the job intimidated by superintendents, board members, and other administrators at higher levels. It is necessary for them to overcome this by learning to manage these relationships comfortably. They must also learn to manipulate the system in order to ensure that personal and site needs are met. In addition, principals in many districts have to achieve an understanding about which of the overwhelming top–down mandates and expectations must be heeded, and which can be safely ignored.

One reason Roxanne was hired as principal was that she was a loyal and committed teacher. When the district told her of its plans to transfer two veteran teachers with histories of unsatisfactory performance to her site, she was torn between advocating for her site and being a "good soldier." She felt that the district was exploiting her, but she was afraid to assert herself. With her coach, Roxanne developed a strategy for dealing with the situation, and role-played the conversations she planned on having with the superintendent.

Balancing Relationships Against Productivity. Principals are often frustrated because they find they don't have enough time for people. In order to survive in their jobs, it is necessary for them to become more efficient in their relationships. They must learn to manage their conversations so they are short but still meet the emotional needs of the participants. There can be a painful tension between the desire to be relaxed and friendly and the need to be task-oriented.

Edward loved people—and was in danger of becoming the most popular but least effective principal in the history of Madrone School. Edward would listen to parents and teachers express their concerns for hours on end. He would chat about family and sports with custodians and trustees without regard to other demands on his time. He was building strong relationships, but he was not attending to other responsibilities; nor was he invested in a vision for his school. As Edward's coach shadowed him for a full day, Edward practiced keeping his conversations short, positive, and productive. He learned to use his daily calendar and tickler files as tools for following through on tasks. As Edward articulated his vision for his school, the strong relationships he had built with his staff served as a powerful base for school improvement.

Not Taking It Personally. Anyone who has been a school leader for any time at all will soon begin to speak of the need to acquire a "thick skin." Learning to manage emotional responses to criticism and conflict is essential to managing personal stress—and, as noted above, to being an effective problem-solver.

José called his coach late on a Friday night. His supervisor had told him that the superintendent was receiving parent and teacher complaints about him. As a result, the superintendent would be conducting a survey and meeting with staff members to assess his performance. José felt attacked, angry, and devastated, all at the same time. But as he discussed this situation with his coach, he came to realize that all of this was a result of his willingness to take on the school's dysfunctional culture. If he mediated his emotions and worked with the superintendent, he could view this review process as an opportunity to expose the school's problems, consolidate his support, and build a mandate for change.

Each of the above issues draws upon professional knowledge and skills, but each also has emotional dimensions. An effective coach must be prepared to address both the cognitive and affective domains in helping a coachee through a variety of challenging situations.

There are a number of excellent sources of useful information for coaches in the area of emotional intelligence. First among them is *Primal Leadership,* by Goleman, Boyatzis, and McKee

(2002). Additional resources are available online. In an article found at https://positivepsychology.com/emotional-intelligence-tests/ (see QR Code 1), the author provides access to several assessments and provides an explanation of why they are important and how they should be used.

QR Code 1
https://positive
psychology.com/
emotional-intelligence-
tests/

*To read a QR code,
you must have a
smartphone or tablet
with a camera. We
recommend that you
download a QR code
reader app that is made
specifically for your
phone or tablet brand.*

WHAT ABOUT LEADER DISPOSITIONS

When working with school leaders the word *dispositions* comes up a lot. The Superintendent may question the Leadership Coach by asking, "do you think Joe has the right disposition to be a high school principal?" The coach often has to ask the Superintendent to clarify what he or she means by disposition. According to Taylor and Wasicsko (2000), dispositions are the personal qualities or characteristics of the individual, such as interests, values, beliefs, attitudes, and modes of adjustments. Borko, Liston, and Whitcomb (2007) took the definition a step further, suggesting dispositions are connected to actions. They describe dispositions as a person's tendencies to act in a given manner reflecting their beliefs and values, values or beliefs that are manifested in a given situation which is predictive of future patterns of behavior.

Principals may have the knowledge and skills they need to lead instruction and manage operations. But if the principal is unable to demonstrate a commitment to students and their learning or effectively communicate with students, parents, and teachers, they will struggle to garner the trust and respect of the school community. Professional dispositions matter. Demonstrating courage, integrity, caring, a strong work ethic, and the ability to think critically (Helm, 2010) are important qualities necessary to lead a school. Borko et al. (2007) take the definition a step further suggesting dispositions are connected to actions. They describe dispositions as a person's tendencies to act in a given manner reflecting their beliefs and values. Collaboration and cultural competence are also necessary skills for the work in schools. Reacting to feedback from a supervisor in a positive manner and acting on it to improve is necessary to grow professionally. Leadership coaches can provide support and resources to assist novice and experienced principals further develop their dispositions.

ISSUES OF CULTURAL PROFICIENCY

In our diverse public schools, the emotional intelligence challenges of leadership are made even more complex by the particular demands of cross-cultural relationships.

Most educators have ample experience and are comfortable working with teachers and parents in the settings in which they have "grown up." But school leaders must learn to navigate the often-unforgiving and diverse cultural and emotional landscapes that exist both inside and outside of the education community. Encounters with new individuals, groups, and situations demand that principals be good listeners, keen observers of emotional response, and effective mediators of their own prejudices and personal communications.

Few jobs make as many demands upon an individual's ability to negotiate across cultures as the principalship. Here are a few examples of cross-cultural challenges we have encountered in our coaching practice:

- The Jewish administrator from the East Coast who had to overcome the suspicions of a large portion of the classified staff in a rural Western community that had little experience with his cultural group.

- A Latino principal who feared that any mistake he made would reflect not only on himself but also on his ethnic group.

- A white female principal who had to develop her own knowledge of and comfort with her school's Asian immigrant community.

Principals who are committed to working with their school communities often struggle with cultural and language barriers. These may exist between the principal and segments of the community, between staff and the community, within the community itself, or across all groups. We are often uncomfortable bringing these issues to the surface. We often make the false assumption that we all share the same cultural understandings and the same commitments around equity.

Lindsey, Robins, and Terrell (1999) outline five elements of cultural proficiency, calling upon school leaders to assess culture, manage the dynamics of difference, institutionalize cultural knowledge, and adapt to and value diversity. School leadership coaching often focuses on each of these elements. We believe that almost all school issues contain cross-cultural elements and suggest that there are both emotional intelligence and cross-cultural aspects to each of the scenarios we present in this book.

Leadership coaches need to be alert to issues of cultural proficiency and emotional intelligence and to have the courage to raise them. Leadership coaches create safe spaces in which to ask questions like "Could race have something to do with your reaction to this angry parent?" Leadership coaches understand that the exercise of the professional knowledge, skills, and abilities outlined by PSEL is grounded in the inter- and intrapersonal.

Reflection: Identify a cross-cultural challenge you have faced in your professional career. What did you learn by facing the challenge? What role did a mentor or other person play in helping you find your way through the situation?

THE CHALLENGE CONTINUES

The principalship seems to become more difficult every year. Many of those who were successful principals at one time—but who have moved on to become professors of educational administration or central office administrators—now question whether they could succeed as principals in today's climate. The complexities of the job, changing socioeconomic realities, ever-increasing expectations, and pressures resulting from the standards and accountability movements have all converged into a perfect storm that now threatens to batter principals and capsize their best efforts. Add increasing political tensions and an international pandemic on top of everything else and the job appears impossible.

It is not only novice principals who are affected. Veterans also need the kind of support that leadership coaching provides. They find themselves in jobs that are very different from the ones they assumed even a few years ago. They must master new areas of knowledge and skills and contend with new challenges to their levels of emotional intelligence and cultural proficiency. In this regard, novice principals may, in fact, be better prepared than their more experienced colleagues to face change and to understand teaching and learning.

As our friend in Figure 2.4 illustrates, a school leader needs the support of both internal and external systems in order to keep standing. A leadership coach can be a critical component of an external support system, and a mentor can be an important internal support.

FIGURE 2.4 ● Support for Educational Professionals

EXTERNAL SUPPORT

INTERNAL SUPPORT

coach

colleagues

family

staff

friends

supervisor

shaky ground

Source: iStock.com/rambo182; iStock.com/robuart; iStock.com/soulcld.

Reflection: What might be other sources of internal and external support for school leaders?

CHAPTER 3

Building Relationships

I t is our opinion that despite different approaches and experience, all coaches must bring certain foundational coaching skills to the table. These include *relationship building; listening, observing, and questioning*; and *giving feedback*.

FOUNDATIONAL COACHING SKILLS

As represented in Figure 3.1, all coaching is centered on increasing the coachee's ability to *set goals* effectively, to *act* in pursuit of those goals, and to *reflect* upon those actions and their impacts. The coachee must be prepared to review and revise goals accordingly, setting new ones when appropriate. As a coach, you must be a skilled listener, observer, and questioner in order to help the coachee clarify context, goals, and impacts of actions taken. You must also cultivate the ability to provide useful feedback that will fuel the coachee's ongoing reflective practice. None of this is possible, however, unless you establish and maintain a relationship with your coachee that is characterized by trust and rapport.

RELATIONSHIP BUILDING

There are few places in life where we are more exposed than in positions of leadership. Our intelligence, our skill, our knowledge, our interpersonal relationships, even our physical appearance and fashion sense are subject to unceasing public scrutiny. Principals are all too familiar with this phenomenon. They are under tremendous pressure to please a number of diverse constituencies, and they are vulnerable on many fronts. They are also extremely busy. It may be a challenge, then, to lead principals to embrace a coaching relationship in which

FIGURE 3.1 ● Foundational Coaching Skills

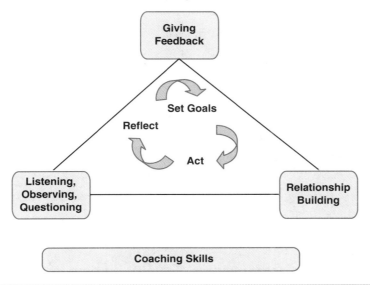

they are asked to slow down, take the time to reflect, and reveal their doubts and failures to a stranger. The same can be said for teachers, who are subject to increasingly high expectations. In this era of social media, everyone in the education enterprise is under scrutiny and often on edge. And of course there is the perception that, "if I need a coach then I must be ineffective." If coaching is to be successful, the coachee must believe that the role of the coach is not to fix something that is wrong. The role of the coach is to nurture professional growth which leads to more effective leadership practices.

Coaching can't happen without a trusting relationship firmly grounded in commitment to help the coachee achieve his or her goals.

> *The role of the coach is granted by the coachee based on trust. Without trust there can be no coaching. Trust will always be at stake during the process of coaching. Trust can increase and become more solid, and it can be taken away. It can be initially gained, then lost and afterwards recovered. Or it can be lost for good. The coach always moves along the thin cord of the coachee's trust. To take for granted the coachee's trust is one of the big mistakes a coach can make.*
> —*Rafael Echeverría and Julio Olalla, authors of* The Art of Ontological Coaching

In her book *Atlas of the Heart*, Brene Brown lists the elements of trust with the initials BRAVING.

Boundaries: You respect my boundaries and when you're not clear about what's okay and not okay, you ask. You're willing to say no.

Reliability: You do what you say you'll do.

Accountability: You own your mistakes, apologize, and make amends.

Vault: You don't share information or experiences that are not yours to share.

Integrity: You choose courage over comfort. You choose what is right over fun, fast or easy.

Nonjudgment: I can ask for what I need, and you can ask for what you need. We can talk about how we feel without judgment.

Generosity: You extend the most generous interpretation possible to the intentions, words, and actions of others.

Brown (2021, p. 192)

Coaching someone requires "*braving*" as detailed above by Brene Brown. It is hard to be nonjudgmental when a principal describes how they handled a situation in a very different way than you would have handled it. It is also essential that a coach operate with integrity and that means protecting information shared and putting it in a personal vault.

BUILDING TRUST

Job one for a coach is to build and maintain trust with the coachee. Powerful coaching simply cannot occur without it. As Echeverría and Olalla make clear, trust is not static; it is established over time, and it must be consciously and consistently nurtured.

Reflection: Think of someone other than a family member or personal friend in whom you have had a high degree of trust. List the characteristics of the individual that supported the establishment of trust.

Trust is an *assessment* that one individual makes about another. Like all assessments, its validity resides in the individual making the judgment. For example, I'm the one who decides whether or not to trust an auto mechanic. Is Joe at the Corner Auto Shop telling me the truth about what's wrong with my car? Is he honest in his billing? Does he know what he's doing? Will he have my car ready when he says he will?

My level of trust may change based upon how I assess Joe's performance over time.

One way to think about trust is as an assessment of *sincerity, reliability,* and *competence.*

When we assess someone's *sincerity,* we are considering whether the individual's actions and internal conversations match their utterances. Do they mean what they say and say what they mean? Here are a few examples of what a coachee might be thinking when assessing a coach's sincerity:

- "My coach says that he is completely here at my service, but I know he's busy. Does he mean it when he says he is available for me 24/7, or is he just being nice?"

- "My coach tells me my problems aren't all that unusual, but she looks worried. Is she really thinking that I'm incompetent?"

- "My coach sure seems like a 'good old boy.' Does he really care about the success of a woman like me?"

In essence, a coach must tell the truth in order to be assessed by the coachee as sincere. We're not saying that a coach should articulate every thought (a likely mistake in most any context!); but what the coach does say must be honest and truly reflect the coach's thoughts, feelings, and intentions. We determine if someone is sincere by matching what they say with their behaviors, including subtle body language, and word choices. A skilled coach is mindful of this and, therefore, always ensures in coaching conversations that words, body language, and actions are congruent.

Another factor in judging whether individuals are trustworthy is their *reliability.* Will they keep their commitments? As a coach, will you actually deliver what you promise? Will you follow through to meet the expectations you have established for yourself? As a coachee assesses a coach's reliability, thoughts such as these may come to mind:

- "My coach says he sometimes socializes with the superintendent, but he assures me that he will keep our coaching conversations confidential. I know he is sincere in his intentions, but can I rely on him to keep his mouth shut about our work together?"

- "She promised to help me plan next week's staff meeting. This is high stakes for me. Is she really going to call when she said she would?"

- "Last time we met, he promised to bring me some articles on block scheduling, but he didn't follow through. So much for him."

Finally, in order to be trusted, an individual must be assessed as *competent*. Coaches must provide evidence that they possess the knowledge and skills required to do the job. We all know people who are completely sincere and quite reliable but not particularly competent, and our trust in them is compromised as a result. A coachee might weigh these sorts of considerations in reflecting upon a coach's competence:

- "My coach has never worked in a school with a high percentage of Black and brown students. Does he have any experience working with the sorts of issues I face here? Will he be able to help me?"
- "She has been away from site administration for six years. Can she help me with all of these new compliance issues?"
- "My coach tells me that I would have been inviting a union grievance if I had followed his advice. I'm not sure that he knows what he's talking about."

Coaches must be clear about the knowledge, skills, and experience they bring to the coaching relationship. They should also remember that their primary job is not to be a competent *principal*—that is the coachee's job—but rather a competent *coach*. It is frequently necessary for coaches to withhold their personal expertise so their coachees can develop individual, internal capacity.

It is important to remember that just as the coach must work to establish and maintain trust with the coachee, the principal must work to establish and maintain trust with the coach as well as with all of the various constituencies the principal serves. An effective coach supports the coachee in being perceived as sincere, reliable, and competent in the principalship.

TRUST BUILDING: BASIC STEPS

Here is a short checklist of the steps taken by effective coaches to build trusting relationships with their coachees.

Demonstrate sincerity by

- Being fully present in the coaching relationship
- Demonstrating personal regard
- Being truthful
- Asking for permission

- ✔ Admitting mistakes
- ✔ Maintaining confidentiality

Demonstrate reliability by

- ✔ Clarifying expectations
- ✔ Keeping commitments
- ✔ Behaving consistently
- ✔ Being available

Demonstrate competence by

- ✔ Letting your coachee know about your expertise and experience
- ✔ Finding outside expertise in cases where you don't possess it
- ✔ Remembering that your job is to be a competent coach, not a competent principal
- ✔ Having high expectations of yourself and of the coaching relationship

A CAVEAT

Sometimes the fear of damaging the relationship or of undermining trust will cause a coach to hold back, to stop short of raising difficult questions or sharing challenging feedback. We remind you that serving as a leadership coach is a critical professional role requiring risk taking and clarity of purpose. It may seem paradoxical, but in our experience, bold coaches have the greatest impact and are most trusted by their coachees.

BUILDING RAPPORT

Being in rapport is the ability to enter someone else's model of the world and let them know that we truly understand their model.
—Michael Brooks, *author of* Instant Rapport

Trust is the ground upon which we build *rapport*, the safe and intimate place that allows for meaningful coaching. We define rapport as a state of harmony and understanding between two people. In a powerful coaching relationship, trust and rapport feed one another and create a space where tough issues can be addressed and where significant growth can occur.

Leadership coaches must consciously work to build rapport, especially in initial meetings with coachees.

As Sonia approached Blackwater Pond Elementary School, she reflected on her initial phone contact with David, her new coachee and the principal of this school. His voice sounded guarded as he talked about his school and his understanding of his involvement with a leadership coach. In spite of her best efforts on the phone, she sensed that he was hesitant about coaching.

Prior to their first meeting, Sonia found out a bit more about the school and David from her district office contact. She learned that he was the third principal in as many years. He had been a successful teacher and then assistant principal at Oliver Middle School for one year. David had been fast-tracked into the principalship, primarily because of a lack of experienced candidates for the position. Black-water was portrayed as an underperforming school with a history of "problem" staff members.

Sonia knew that her first few moments with David would be important in establishing the coaching relationship. As David appeared in the reception area of the outer office, she stood up to greet him and extended her hand.

RAPPORT BUILDING: BASIC STEPS

Many people who "hit it off" right away do so naturally and unconsciously. However, rapport can be built consciously by using deliberate verbal and nonverbal communication strategies. Because rapport building is essential to success in the private sector (no, that salesman may not really be all *that* interested in your kids), there has been a fair amount of research done in this area that can be applied to coaching school leaders. As you build a close relationship with your coachees, attend to the following steps.

Discover and share personal and professional connections. In American culture and in the busy world of school leadership, it is usually our impulse to get down to business and to do it right *now*. Some of us are hesitant to take the time to get to know our colleagues on a personal basis, to learn about their private lives and to find common friends, experiences, and interests. While coaching sessions should not be social time, we do encourage coaches to know and be known by their coachees on a personal level.

Be curious and encourage curiosity with your coachee. It is okay to admit that you don't have a recipe or solution for every problem that may come up in a coaching conversation.

What you want is to initiate a conversation that encourages curiosity and interests regarding the challenge to evoke creative problem-solving. Asking the coachee to ask questions may not elicit this curiosity. You may have to "prime the pump" according to George Loewenstein in his article "The Psychology of Curiosity" (1994). By providing resources, exploring, possible solutions, and asking questions, the coach can provoke interest and curiosity.

Be fully present in the conversation. As a coach, it is your responsibility to give your full attention to your coachee. You must tune out both internal and external distractions: the argument you had with your teenager that morning, the bad traffic on your way to your appointment, the smell of mildew emanating from the carpet in the principal's office—all of these must be shut out as you focus only on your coachee.

Be aware of your body language. Your eyes, face, posture, and gestures all communicate at least as much as your words. When we watch two individuals converse, we can see their rapport in the way they lean toward one another, in their eye contact, and in the dance of their gestures. In *Instant Rapport*, Michael Brooks suggests that rapport can actually be built by subtly mirroring an individual's gestures to establish a harmony that will extend into conversation and relationship.

Listen impeccably. We will talk more about listening in the next section, but here it must be said that active listening is critical to building rapport. The pioneering psychiatrist Karl Menninger is credited with pointing out, "Listening is a magnetic and strange thing, a creative force. The friends who listen to us are the ones we move toward. When we are listened to, it creates us, makes us unfold and expand."

Michael Brooks (1989) suggests we can build rapport by listening for and speaking to a person's way of processing information, which he claims falls into one of three categories: visual, auditory, and kinesthetic. When we build rapport through impeccable listening, we try to get ourselves into the skin of the other person and understand fully the way in which he or she is experiencing the world.

Communicate acceptance. It's impossible to feel rapport with someone whom you experience as even slightly threatening—or who conveys disdain, rejection, superiority, or contempt. Manifest acceptance is the foundation of rapport—and of all that is positive in relationships.

Sonia smiled at David and let him know she was pleased to meet him. She let him take the lead in the flow of the conversation, giving him her full attention as he showed her the way to his office. Once there, Sonia sat down, being careful to keep an open body position (arms relaxed and uncrossed, body directly facing the speaker). She remained focused on David and what he was saying. She listened intently to David as he described his school, nodding and using verbal responses such as "Uh hum . . . I see . . . Umm." She asked him a bit about his personal background and discovered a few things they had in common. They had attended the same MA program; they both had children; and both had taught middle school in the southern part of the state.

As the conversation proceeded, Sonia could see David relax and become more open and engaged in the discussion. He was less hesitant in his speech patterns and more animated as he described his family and past experiences. David looked directly at Sonia, smiled, and even laughed a few times as he described his feelings about his new assignment. At the end of their appointment, David asked, "So, when can you come back?"

As Sonia left David's office, she was confident that she had begun to establish rapport and trust, and she felt David was more open to having a coach. She had consciously done more listening than speaking. She had focused on attending to what he was saying and how he was saying it. At times she carefully used a few mirroring techniques and observed that he responded well to these. Sonia left the school looking forward to her work with David, satisfied that the time she had spent today building rapport with him would provide a solid foundation for coaching.

Exercise: The next time you are at a party or a mixer, approach a stranger and strike up a conversation. Make a conscious effort to establish rapport. Observe yourself and your partner throughout the conversation. What did you talk about? What did your body language communicate? What elements of your conversation contributed to your success or lack of success at establishing rapport?

CHAPTER 4

Listening, Observing, and Questioning

Powerful coaching is grounded in the basic skills of listening, observing, and questioning. The coach is a different observer, able to help the coachee see new possibilities in an existing situation by providing new data and perspectives.

My coach has this uncanny ability to track what I am talking about on so many levels. I have come to notice that she is doing much more than just listening to what I am saying. She watches me carefully to see how I am feeling and what is going on below the surface. When we are in the middle of talking about some problem I am facing, she is able to hold my issue in the greater context of what she knows about me and where I have been and where I am going.

—*Antonio, second-year principal at Chavez Middle School*

Listening, observing, and questioning are complex, multidimensional processes. In even the simplest conversations, we attend to a speaker's words, vocal inflections, gestures, and facial expressions and to our own emotional reactions to and interpretations of the speaker. This broad spectrum of inputs makes up the gestalt of our listening.

By now, the notion of "active listening" is a cliché: Do you *hear* what we are saying? However, the fact that we *talk* about listening does not mean that we educators are good listeners. Nor are we particularly good observers. It is interesting to note that efforts to drive school improvement by "data-based decision making" are all about improving our performance as observers and listeners.

We tend to think of communication as the act of transmitting and receiving information. This model may work between computers passing digital information back and forth without distorting or losing data. But humans are not hardwired, and all communication is filtered through our listening. It is shaped by our biases, experiences, intentions, and interpretations.

LISTENING TO WORDS

Listening includes attention to context and to nonverbal data. However, words alone convey huge amounts of information, information that is often underutilized. As you listen carefully to verbal communication, it is sometimes helpful to imagine you are reading a transcript rather than watching an individual speak. What are the facts, assumptions, and details embedded in the speaker's story? What do the speaker's word choices convey? Are the spoken messages free of generalizations? Free of bias? Of blame and finger pointing? Is the speaker reasoned in the choice of words used to describe the event or the person involved? Are there patterns of language or comments that tell us about the speaker's way of thinking?

Let's look at the comments of one new principal—we'll call her Joan—about some of her teachers:

I think things are going well overall. I do have a bunch of older teachers who are constantly saying that things aren't fair. They want me to make the decisions but only the decisions they agree with and not the ones they do not agree with. They want me to be like the last principal—a bit top–down and directive.

Reflection: What do Joan's words tell you about her way of thinking and interacting?

There are only four sentences in Joan's statement. We have no nonverbal information and know nothing about the school except for what is conveyed in the statement. However, these four sentences hint at some significant issues that might emerge in working with this principal.

Joan speaks in generalities ("things are going well," "a bunch," "constantly saying," "they want"). She seems to be making broad judgments. Is she backing up her opinions with data?

Joan seems to have a dismissive attitude, referring to "older teachers" and "they" and to the former principal as "top-down."

We can see the beginning of an unhealthy polarization here, an alienation between Joan and at least a portion of her staff.

ASSERTIONS AND ASSESSMENTS

Joan has constructed a story about her school, a story that is built upon a series of judgments. If Joan is like most people much of the time, she has confused her interpretations with reality. She will proceed to interact with her staff under the illusion that her story is *the* story. A powerful coach will help Joan recognize that her story is not necessarily reality. Rather, it is an interpretation; being open to other interpretations might open Joan to new and more productive ways of engaging with her staff.

In our coaching practice, we have found it helpful to be able to make the distinction between two types of speech known as *assertions* and *assessments*. The characteristics of these are derived from the work of linguist John Searle and philosopher Rafael Echeverría. They are among a group of contemporary thinkers who have taught us about the generative power of language.

We recognize that some readers may have trouble with this use of the words *assertion* and *assessment*. Assessment, in particular, carries a particular meaning for most educators in regard to its application to testing. For the purpose of our discussion, we ask you to suspend any preconceived definitions of these terms and entertain the ones we introduce here.

Searle (1969) maintains that assertions and assessments are two of the small number of basic speech acts that can be found in all languages in all cultures. Assertions describe facts that can be corroborated by a witness. Here are some examples:

- "It is 73°F in this room."
- "Susana scored 1,500 points on the SAT."
- "Four parents attended the last site council meeting."
- "Three students did not complete the assignment."

Each of these statements is either true or false, measured by some kind of commonly held standard (such as degrees Fahrenheit). They reside outside of the speaker in the sense that they do not represent the speaker's opinion or judgment. Instead, they are attempts to describe an objective reality.

Contrast the above assertions with these assessments:

- "It is hot in this room."
- "Susana is smart."
- "Parents here just don't want to get involved."
- "John has low expectations of his students."

Assessments are not true or false by any objective measure. Rather, they are judgments or opinions. They reside in the speaker. For example, when I say, "It's hot in this room," I am commenting on my internal experience. Assessments are speech acts that change our experience of reality and shape our future actions. They impact the way in which we behave. They are the fabric from which our interpretations are constructed.

There is nothing wrong with making assessments. In fact, we have to make them in order to function effectively in the world. However, we get in trouble when we confuse our assessments, or interpretations, with assertions, or facts. Useful assessments are well grounded in assertions; harmful assessments are often pulled out of thin air. Joan has confused her assessments with assertions. She has made a string of assessments that will shape her actions and determine the ways in which others will react to her. When she states, "I do have a bunch of older teachers who are constantly saying that things aren't fair," she paints the picture of a crew of cranky veterans who are going to get in her way. Her language includes a number of assessments ("bunch," "older," "constantly") and no clear assertions. An effective coach might help Joan to unpack her statement and arrive at new interpretations.

COACH: Joan, who are these teachers, and what is their complaint?

JOAN: Sandy, a teacher who has been here for a long time, told me that she and a couple of the other veteran teachers are not happy because we are changing reading programs. She says they invested a lot of time in developing their literature-based program, and they don't want to give it up.

COACH: So we are talking about a small group of teachers who are hesitant to give up a program that they have made a personal investment in. Have you thought about ways in which you can harness their experience with and interest in literature-based programs to help you to move them toward your literacy initiative?

In addition to our assessments of other people and external experiences, the assessments we make about ourselves can have a huge impact on our effectiveness. In the Resource section at the end of this book, we offer a worksheet that will guide you or a coachee through a reflection on self-assessment (see Resource A.2).

SEPARATING ASSERTIONS FROM ASSESSMENTS: BASIC STEPS

Coaches can guide their coachees to an awareness of assessments and assertions by:

- Listening for situations in which the coachee is confusing assessments with assertions.

- Helping the coachee ground and reevaluate assessments by asking three questions:
  - Assessment for the sake of what?
  - Assessment against what standards?
  - Assessment based on what assertions?

- Pointing out self-assessments, the coachee may make that are not well-grounded and, therefore, are likely to limit possibilities.

NARRATIVES

Listening for and intervening in a coachee's use of assertions and assessments is a powerful coaching tool. We encourage coaches to teach their coachees these distinctions and to help them to develop the habits of mind that allow them to examine their own use of assertions and assessments.

A related and perhaps even more vital tool for coaches is the habit of listening for, naming, questioning, and helping coachees to reshape narratives. Narratives can be understood as stories that are grounded in assessments, stories that will justify and shape future assessments, and future actions.

LISTENING FOR AND INTERVENING IN NARRATIVES

To be a human being is to live in a complex, multidimensional welter of inputs and interactions, all experienced through the lenses of our own perceptual abilities, our own biases, needs, reactions, histories, and inclinations and abilities to act. We make sense of it all by constructing stories, interpretations, generalizations that allow us to organize all that we experience, to predict the future, and guide our actions. In our professional lives, we are surrounded by narratives of minor consequence... *the kids are always hyper after they have sugar*... and major consequence... *union leadership only cares about members, not about our students.*

Over the past few decades, the power of narratives (and the use of the word "narratives" in the public discourse) in manipulating perception and action has been recognized, and we don't have to look far to find examples of stories constructed by marketers and politicians deliberately constructed to serve their interests. *Matt Damon tells us "fortune favors the brave ... buy crypto," Putin tells us that there is no legitimate Ukrainian nationality.*

Effective teachers build narratives within their classrooms that inspire student achievement. *We are a family and we care about each other and treat each other well. Everyone here matters.* Effective principals do the same. *We are making a difference in our students' lives, and in our community, one reading lesson at a time.* Effective teachers and principals know the power of more granular stories that inspire and are examples of success. *Maria is in our school Hall of Fame. She is a neurosurgeon who came here from Nicaragua as a second grader.*

Our behaviors are also shaped by internal narratives, stories, and interpretations we tell ourselves but may not always share with others. *I'm terrible at math ... my principal doesn't respect me because I am so young. I'm here because of my commitment to social justice but for the rest of them this is just a job.*

Here are some examples of narratives, their potential impacts, and alternative narratives that open up positive possibilities.

NARRATIVE: The parents at this school don't support their children or education. They don't show up at open house and don't ensure that their kids do their homework.

IMPACT: Given this story, a teacher or principal is likely to expect very little from parents and their children. An alternative narrative might sound something like this: *Many parents at this school are struggling economically and are working multiple jobs to make ends meet. They have made major sacrifices coming to this country for their children's futures. We need to reach out to them on their terms in order to build on their commitment.*

NARRATIVE:	*The district office doesn't understand the needs at our site. They just keep pushing down mandates without understanding how they impact us. All they care about are short-term gains in test scores.*
IMPACT:	A teacher or principal locked into this narrative is likely to feel like a victim of the bureaucracy and is not likely to embrace innovation and shared professional practice. An alternative narrative might sound something like this: *The district leadership shares our commitment to raising student achievement but may not fully understand some of our challenges on the ground. I need to find a way to help them to understand our concerns.*
NARRATIVE:	*As an African-American leader, I am judged by a higher standard than my white colleagues and negative judgments end up as reflection not only upon me but upon my race. I'm stuck in a no-win situation.*
IMPACT:	Like many narratives, this one may be rooted in reality, yet such a narrative can easily inhibit a leader's willingness to take risks and to advocate for students and community. An alternative narrative might sound something like this: *My colleagues and community have high expectations because they care about our students, as do I. As a leader committed to having a positive impact upon our students, I expect to take some criticism and I recognize that racial bias is a presence in my professional life. This doesn't feel fair, but it is a price I am willing to pay in order to make a difference.*

At a more basic level, narratives often take the form of generalizations or assumptions that are not grounded, in fact, but that may drive behaviors. Examples include statements like "*My students are not well prepared for algebra*" when in any class there are like to be some students who are prepared and some who are not, or "*The teachers at my school do not have a high enough level of trust to participate in peer observations,*" when, in fact, trust is not a prerequisite for conducting peer observations but rather peer observations are a way of building trust.

An effective coach listens for the narratives that a coachee brings to his or her professional performance and shares his or her observations along the way. A coach may ask clarifying questions like "*When you refer to your students, do you mean all of them? What percentage, or which of your students does this apply to?*" A coach may explicitly point out a narrative, explore its implications, and suggest an alternative narrative. In this example, Principal Mary takes a coaching stance in working with teacher Rob:

ROB (Teacher):	I don't have time in my day to teach the science curriculum. I'm under too much pressure to teach the mathematics and language arts curriculum.
MARY (Principal):	*What are the implications of not getting around to science?*
ROB:	*Well, kids aren't going to do well on the science section on the state test.*
MARY:	*True. And they are going to miss out on some important content and won't be ready to pick up on science next year. And, you know, for some kids, science is really engaging and motivating.*
ROB:	*But I really have a hard time getting to science because I have to get these guys going into English Language Arts.*
MARY:	*Rob, you are telling yourself that you don't have time for science, and that ELA is a priority. But there is a different way of approaching this that might turn it into a "win-win." Science is a fabulous vehicle for teaching and reinforcing language arts. How about approaching this from the understanding that weaving science into your ELA instruction is a great opportunity, a way to motivate your kids, make teaching more interesting, and to improve achievement in both ELA and science?*
ROB:	*That all sounds good, but I don't have time to create a new curriculum.*
MARY:	*Not necessary. Let me get some resources for you and get you into Sue Smith's fourth grade classroom at Wilson. She really has this going on.*

It is worth noting that effective coaching and supervision are best embedded in a shared narrative. *We are engaging in this professional development because being an educator is all about continuing learning and all of us, myself included, are full on members of professional learning communities* is going to be much better received than the narrative *we need to participate in this professional development because we are not doing a great job in mathematics and the district has committed to this program.*

NONVERBAL COMMUNICATION

Albert Mehrabian (1972) has conducted research demonstrating that only about 7% of the emotional meaning of a message is communicated through the exchange of words. Some 38% is communicated by vocal intonation, and the remaining 55% is expressed through gestures, posture, facial expressions, and other physical cues.

In this digital era, we still spend huge amounts of money bringing people together in the same physical space. We may accomplish a lot in our abstract, digital worlds, but we remain (thank goodness!) animals that rely on proximity, on sight, smell, touch, and a wealth of other subtle cues essential to communication. Among other things, the COVID-19 pandemic taught us that for many, if not most, communications, physical proximity makes a difference.

The ability to interpret nonverbal cues is the hallmark of a truly skilled listener. Paying attention to *how* a message is communicated is often more telling and informative than the actual content of the message. When attending to nonverbal communication, the listener watches facial expressions and body language for clues about the internal state of the speaker. Listening for the speaker's vocal inflections (monotone, tense, excited) and the rate of speech (rapid, calm, agitated, hesitant) provides additional clues. What is the body position of the speaker? Closed? Relaxed? Fidgeting?

Let's visit a few principals and "listen" to what they might be communicating to their coaches:

- As Maria walks out to meet her coach on Monday morning, she is moving slowly and sighs to herself as she enters the outer office. Although she says, "I am glad to see you," her voice is slow and heavy. Her coach wonders what has affected Maria's mood. She knows that one of her goals in today's session will be to understand Maria's effect.

- Lance is very quiet in this initial meeting. He is not forthcoming in responding to his coach's questions, often answering in just a few words. Although cordial, he sits with his arms crossed in front of his chest and does not make consistent eye contact. The coach predicts that she is going to have to do some groundwork to win Lance's trust and buy-in to the coaching process.

- John is friendly and outgoing and typically uses humor during his meetings with his coach. He is relaxed and frequently shares personal stories about his family. When his coach asks him a question about difficult school issues, he usually reflects and takes his time responding. He often expresses his appreciation for the opportunity to confide in a "safe" person. But today he is short-tempered. He interrupts the coach and has gotten up and left the office three different times to give his secretary tasks. He is playing with a pen on his desk and seems not to be focusing on the topic at hand. John's coach shares his observations with John, leading to a discussion of a stressful issue that has arisen at his school.

- As Tony observes the staff meeting at his coachee Richard's school, he is pleased at the outset to see that Richard has taken him up on his suggestion to have teachers present some key agenda items as a means to develop and strengthen shared leadership. Then Tony begins to notice that Richard is having a hard time keeping his feelings to himself about what is being shared by teachers. He frowns and moves around in his seat in an agitated manner. He is also taking notes and making comments to the assistant principal seated at his side. Tony shares these observations with Richard, and they discuss the possible impacts of Richard's behaviors.

In each of these cases, nonverbal messages may be much more important than the coachees' utterances.

 Exercise: Flip on the TV and watch an interview show with the sound off. How much information can you gather just by watching gestures and facial expressions?

OBSERVING EMOTION AND MOOD

Our work would be easy if it only required us to master organizational, operational, and pedagogical matters. But because the business of coaching and supervising educators happens in a human context, we must be prepared to observe and address affective issues, the domains of mood and emotion.

While emotion and mood are closely related, there is a distinction between the two concepts. Emotions are immediate and are often triggered by events. They can be hard for us to control. Daniel Goleman (1998; Goleman et al., 2002) reminds us that effective leaders mediate their emotional reactions and are highly conscious of the impact their emotional states have on others.

Mood is related to emotion, but is a more enduring sensibility. Because mood is a deeper and more durable state, it has a huge impact upon an individual or organization's efficacy. Think about the differences in mood between a staff meeting at a school that is coming together around common goals and one at a school that is mired in resistance to change. Mood is a predisposition to emotion and action.

Individuals operate in moods that leave them inclined to react in particular ways. A principal who is in a depressed and discouraged mood—such as Maria, in the example above—may be less than enthusiastic when, for instance, a special needs student steps in the door to register for school. If such a mood persists, it will pervade the school and significantly harm the culture there. Leaders help to shape the moods of their organizations.

Because moods and emotions exist in individuals and in organizations, effective coaches are alert to the emotional state of both the coachee and the coachee's context. These coaches observe the coachee's emotions and mood, monitor the emotions and mood in his/her professional context, and are prepared to intervene in both if need be.

Emotion is very much grist for the mill of coaching. Powerful coaches observe the emotional states of their coachees and how those emotions are experienced by others. A coach's own emotional reaction to a coachee is valuable data in the coaching process. In doing so, they take advantage of what psychoanalysts call *countertransference*, the coach's own emotional involvement in the interaction with the coachee as a source of insight.

GATHERING DATA, OBSERVING THE CONTEXT

While we have focused primarily on how coaches listen to and observe their coachees, it is important to note that coaches cannot rely upon one-on-one conversations with coachees as their only source of data. Remember that the power of coaching lies in our ability to be different observers and help our coachees develop new interpretations and possibilities. We must apply our listening and observing skills to other sources of information, including:

- 360° survey instruments (a sample is included in Resource C.3) that solicit feedback from a coachee's supervisors, subordinates, peers, and community;

- situations in which coachees are doing "real work," such as facilitating staff meetings, conferencing with parents, and supervising teachers;

- evidence of school effectiveness, including test data, classroom observations, and surveys; and

- coachee logs, reflections, and diaries.

RECURSIVE LISTENING

Recursive listening is defined as the act of *listening to listening*. There is a metacognitive dimension to effective listening and observing. Coaching requires the ability to focus completely upon the coachee and his or her environment. As coaches, we must be fully present as listeners and observers.

Good listeners learn to shut down the inner voice that is framing a response instead of attending to a speaker. They cultivate the ability to ignore their own grumbling stomachs and quiet their internal distractors ("I need to remember to call the office after this appointment."). Even as we shut down irrelevant internal noise, we can learn a great deal about our coachees and ourselves by *listening to our listening*.

In the kind of simple one-on-one coaching interaction illustrated in Figure 4.1, the coach must ask:

- What do I hear and observe from the coachee (A)?

- How is the coachee listening and observing me (B)?

- What can I learn from attending to my own listening (C)?

FIGURE 4.1 ● Reciprocal Listening

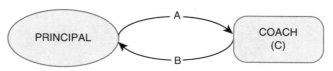

FIGURE 4.2 ● Multilevel Listening

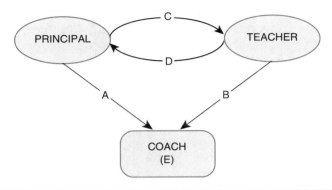

In other words, in a coaching conversation, the coach clearly can learn a lot by attending to the coachee's communication. The coach can also learn something about the coachee's disposition and skills by observing the ways in which the coachee listens to her coach. In listening to our own listening, we ask ourselves these sorts of questions:

- What is my emotional reaction to this coachee? Does she make me like her and want to engage with her? If I am reacting in this way to her, how might others react?

- Which of my negative and positive biases and "hot buttons" does this coachee trigger?

- As I observe myself in this conversation, what does my deep intuition tell me might be going on here?

Taking the notion of recursive listening just a bit further, Figure 4.2 illustrates the kind of complex listening that might take place as a coach observes a conversation between a teacher and a principal.

In this example, the coach's listening and observing skills must extend through five dimensions:

1. What do I hear and observe from the principal (A)?

2. What do I hear and observe from the teacher (B)?

3. What is the principal hearing and observing from the teacher (C)?

4. What is the teacher hearing and observing from the principal (D)?

5. What can I learn from observing my own listening (E)?

QUESTIONING

In the coaching relationship, questioning can serve both to inform the coach and to influence the coachee. In the first case, questioning is one of the ways in which a coach gathers information that will help to assess a coachee's needs and context. In the second, questioning is a powerful tool for helping a coachee clarify his own thinking, develop new interpretations, and discover new possibilities.

Regardless of their specific purpose, effective questions generally share some common characteristics, examples of which are included in Table 4.1.

Exercise: This exercise is to be conducted with a close friend or family member *only*. Ask the question, "Do you love me?" ten different ways, conveying ten different meanings. Use only these four words.

As this exercise will illustrate, effective questions are constructed of words, certainly, but also of nonverbal cues.

TABLE 4.1 • Six Characteristics of Effective Questions

EFFECTIVE QUESTIONS ARE	THEY SOUND LIKE THIS	NOT LIKE THIS
Open ended	Tell me about your teaching experience.	Where did you teach?
	What do you think about. . .?	Do you believe in. . .?
Invitational	It would be great to hear about. . .	Why on earth would you. . .?
	Would you consider. . .?	Why don't you...?
Specific	How often does she. . .?	Does she . . . much?
	What does it look like when. . .?	What will happen if. . .?
Evocative	What might this mean?	What does this mean?
	Let's speculate about. . .	What will happen if. . .?
Positively or neutrally biased	What might you learn from this?	What's up with. . .?
	Tell me what you were thinking.	What did you think would happen?
Challenge assessments	What evidence do you have that. . .?	What is wrong with. . .?
	How could that be interpreted differently?	What's your feeling about. . .?

Remember that questions do more than issue a request for a response; they communicate a great deal about the questioner. Effective questioning is inextricably linked to effective listening, and because of this, it is key to the relationship between coach and coachee.

We will return to this topic in Chapter 7, where we will explore mediational questioning, a form of questioning that helps the coachee shift his or her ways of doing and being.

BIAS IN LISTENING, OBSERVING, AND QUESTIONING

What do you see in Figure 4.3?

Most people who have grown up in developed countries see two people, perhaps an adult and a child, standing outside or inside a building. Anthropologists found that individuals living in the African bush were likely to see a mother with a package on her head, standing with a child under a tree.

This illustrates the reality that each of us brings a unique set of biases to our observations, and every coach brings personal points of view to the coaching role. This is not necessarily a negative phenomenon, but it is something that we must keep in mind as coaches. Our gender, culture, age, and experiences all shape the ways in which we perceive our coachees and their contexts. These attributes also influence the ways in which we are perceived by them.

We see what we are attuned to, and sometimes miss extraordinarily important data. This is well illustrated by the selective attention experiment by Daniel Simons you can find using QR Code 2.

QR Code 2
https://www.youtube.com/watch?v=vJG698U2Mvo

FIGURE 4.3 ● What Do You See?

A coach who has spent most of her career in elementary schools will see high schools from a different perspective than an individual who has done most of her work at the secondary level. A Latino coach may bring a different perspective to issues of student discipline than an African-American coach. A male coach may be received differently by a female coachee than a female coach would be.

We claim that one of the fundamental strengths a coach brings to the coaching relationship is the fact that he or she is a different observer, with a different perspective. The biases brought by individual coaches to their listening, observing, and questioning can be a source of power and richness in coaching—as long as the coach is aware of the ways in which they are manifest and is open in sharing those biases with the coachee.

In Resource A.1, we have included a worksheet designed to help coaches think about the inherent biases they bring to their coaching relationships.

CHAPTER 5

Providing Feedback

The third basic skill a coach must have is the ability to provide useful feedback to a coachee, feedback that will fuel ongoing reflective practice.

Effective feedback gives an individual or group clear, concise verbal and/or written data about events, patterns or conditions of behavior or organizational culture for the purpose of improved performance. Providing feedback is a process which includes observing an action or system and gathering information about it for the purpose of evaluation or corrections.

—Patricia McLagan and Peter Krembs, *authors of* On the Level: Performance Communication That Works

As a different observer, the coach is able to see what the coachee cannot. Coaches often share observations by providing direct feedback. Just when and how we provide this feedback depends upon the coachee's readiness to hear what we have to say. It hinges on both our relationship with our coachee and the coachee's capacity to receive and apply the feedback.

Anyone who has been successful in a sport knows the power of an observant coach. The golf pro who suggests a slightly different grip, the swimming coach who points out a too-frequent breathing pattern—both draw your attention to subtle behaviors that are invisible to you but if changed can significantly improve your performance.

Educators receive feedback regularly, but it is almost always indirect and informal. It accompanies everyday interactions, events, and accomplishments. Strong educators are attuned to this informal feedback and use it to shape their practice.

Unfortunately, formal feedback systems are very weak in most school settings. Most principal supervision models consist of one or two meetings a year and an annual summative report. Most teachers might experience a few walk-throughs by their supervisors and a formal write-up every few years. Supervisors often don't provide their subordinates with meaningful formative feedback. In addition, feedback from a supervisor, however accurate, is colored by the supervisor's authority.

Feedback from a coach is different because a coach has no formal power in relation to the coachee. The feedback a coach shares with a coachee is confidential and poses no threat to job security. It is safe, it serves the coachee's best interests, and it is all about improving practice. A coachee can challenge a coach's feedback and remain confident that an issue raised by a coach will not wind up on a year-end evaluation. We'll talk about the value of a supervisor's feedback in Chapter 12.

 Reflection: Think of a time when someone gave you feedback that helped you to be better at something. What were the characteristics of the feedback and the way in which it was delivered that made it effective?

CHARACTERISTICS OF EFFECTIVE FEEDBACK

Feedback from a coach can be powerful, helping individuals to reflect upon and improve their practice. Or it can backfire, producing defensiveness and undermining the coach/coachee relationship. Effective feedback is likely to have the following characteristics:

It is specific and grounded in evidence.

THIS	NOT THIS
Your failure rate for African American students in algebra is 35%.	You are not serving kids of color well at this school.
Let's count the number of students who are on task during our observation.	We saw poor student engagement in that classroom.

It is tied to explicit goals, expectations, and/or standards.

THIS	NOT THIS
Your school plan calls for 80% of your students to be college eligible upon graduation.	I know that you are focusing on equity this year.
What is your expectation in relation to implementation of engagement strategies?	I'm sure that Ms. Jones can do a better job.

It is linked to impact on teaching and learning.

THIS	NOT THIS
When students fail algebra they are cut off from a college eligible path.	You are not going to meet your goals here.
How is Ms. Jones' classroom management impacting her students and her team?	That was a disappointing classroom visit.

It is bold but never mean-spirited.

THIS	NOT THIS
What is your sense of urgency about this situation?	How long will you allow this pattern to continue?
What would effective feedback and support to Ms. Jones look like?	I'm surprised that you have not held Ms. Jones accountable for her poor classroom management.

In addition, effective feedback:

- Communicates that the coach or supervisor has the coachee's best interests at heart and believes that growth can occur.

- Provides an opportunity, where appropriate, for conversation about issues of personal style, equity, dispositions, and relationships.

- Is delivered, when possible, in an invitational manner and at a time and place conducive to a safe conversation.

- It is not personal; it focuses upon practices, behaviors, evidence, and impact.

- It is offered with the opportunity to reflect. Note that, as in some of the examples above, feedback can be implied in questions. Feedback is implied in what you choose to notice or not, in your body language, in many ways.

Ideally, the coachee should share in determining the goal, type, and purpose of the feedback. When a coachee asks you to share your observations, it is an invitation to powerful coaching as well as an indication that the coachee is a committed learner.

At times, you may find that you need to seek permission to share your feedback with a coachee. Assuming you have a trusting relationship with your coachee, be bold in offering feedback.

Would you mind if I shared a few observations about the conversation I just observed between you and your assistant? I noticed some things that may be contributing to that tension you were mentioning the last time I was here.

Here you have asked permission and linked the permission to your purpose in providing the feedback. By providing feedback to address an expressed need, you are laying the foundation for providing more personal feedback at a later date as the need arises.

Provide feedback that is aligned with coachee and school needs. Just as a swim coach is standing alongside the pool, stopwatch in hand, looking for the change in breathing patterns that could improve a swimmer's time, a leadership coach is constantly scanning for data that could provide the coachee with feedback of strategic importance.

For example, you have noted that your coachee complains repeatedly of being overwhelmed. You have observed that she hesitates to delegate basic clerical tasks to her office staff and does not share leadership effectively with her assistant principal or teachers. As you begin to help her develop a process for writing this year's school plan, you realize that this conversation will also allow you to provide her with feedback about her hesitancy to delegate and to offer instruction to help her delegate the tasks necessary to complete the school planning process.

You know, there is something I have noticed this year which I would like to share with you. My observations are about how you appear to delegate tasks and share responsibilities. Since we are talking about how to make the planning process successful, this might be a good time to share some observations and ideas with you. What do you say?

Effective feedback is grounded in data. The coach's goal is to provide the coachee with assertions (data) that will lead the coachee to make an assessment that in turn will lead to a change in behavior. The more concrete and specific the data, the easier it will be for your coachee to see and hear what the data suggest. Assessments in and of themselves—"You don't do a very good job of delegating"—don't make for effective feedback. Assertions do.

COACH: "I've noticed you are doing a number of tasks that other principals delegate. For example, you are keeping the school's books and facilitating all of the grade level meetings."

PRINCIPAL: "Everybody else is so busy, I feel like I have to take those things on."

COACH: "Now you are talking about a school planning process in which you will be doing the writing on your own. What might be some of the consequences of that approach?"

PRINCIPAL: "Aside from grinding myself into the ground? I suppose there might be less buy-in."

COACH: "Possibly. I have observed that you really hesitate to share responsibilities. I'd like to explore your reasons for this pattern and help you to set up some mechanisms that will make it easier for you to delegate. A good vehicle for this might be around the school plan since you already understand the limitations of doing it alone."

As you look to provide feedback, remember that your data must be objective and your assessments firmly grounded in assertions. Your work as a coach requires you to be a neutral observer of the coachee and the events surrounding the coachee. A statement such as "You are allowing a few people to dominate your staff meeting" is not likely to be as well received as "During your meeting, I heard four of the twenty-two teachers speak, two of them three times each. It appeared that you made a decision based on those four voices. How do you think the rest of the staff interpreted this exchange?"

Provide feedback comparing planned outcomes to actual outcomes. Because coaching is an ongoing process, it allows us to meet with coachees to discuss their planning for activities or events, to observe them, and to debrief with them afterward. During the initial planning stage, a coach can help a coachee clarify goals as well as identify the kinds of feedback the coachee would like to receive.

COACH: "So, we are going to be observing Mike in the classroom today, and I am also going to observe your post-observation conference. Could you share what you hope to accomplish with Mike through this process?"

PRINCIPAL: "Mike and I have been talking about the number of kids who are failing his algebra class. I want to bring him around to recognizing the need to do more direct instruction and to provide more individualized help to some of his students."

COACH: "What would you like me to watch for in the post-observation conference?"

PRINCIPAL: "I want to get Mike to see that he has to change what he is doing. In the past when I have conferenced with him and pointed out these sorts of problems, he has become very defensive. Those conferences never went anywhere."

Link outcomes to behaviors. Feedback that is framed as "when you did X, it produced Y" is very persuasive.

PRINCIPAL: "Mike seemed OK with the observation. I'm surprised he didn't realize that group of kids was off task."

COACH: "You helped him to see what is going on in the class, and he did not respond defensively. When you showed him the data you had collected on student engagement and completion of the work, he came to his own conclusions."

Feedback is more likely to be received positively when it is delivered through acknowledgment of a coachee's areas of strength. Coachees look to their coaches for reassurance and support. They are more open to growth when feedback is not perceived as a challenge to their competence.

COACH: "You collected data in Mike's class that clearly illustrated the experience of the at-risk kids in there. You presented him with lots of strategies he could use with the class."

PRINCIPAL: "Then why was it so hard for me to get him to commit to any next steps?"

COACH: "Is it possible that because you had collected and shared so much observation data, and have so much expertise around teaching strategies, that he felt overwhelmed? You could be a tremendous resource to Mike, but you are having a hard time getting through to him. Is it possible that he is feeling intimidated by you?"

Pay attention to timing. Feedback needs to be given when it is likely to be received. Poorly timed feedback may fall on deaf ears or may erode the trusting relationship the coach has worked so hard to build. There may be times when the coach observes a behavior that is working against the coachee but decides to hold off on sharing this observation. Powerful coaching occurs over time, and it may be weeks or months before the right opportunity arises to present sensitive feedback. The deeper the relationship between coach and coachee, the stronger the trust and the bolder the coach can be. Feedback and relationship are mutually reinforcing factors. Bold and appropriate feedback properly delivered builds the coaching relationship, and this allows for the continued sharing of effective feedback.

Positive feedback is important. Feedback has the potential to inspire our coachees. Look for opportunities to recognize their effective practices and strengths. Life as a professional educator can be a tough and lonely business, and coachees often need the reinforcement that coaches can provide through positive feedback. Keep positive feedback specific, grounded in solid evidence and focused upon impact. Global praise will do little to inspire and support. It is much like fast food—satisfying for a short time but with little nutritional value for the long haul.

BUILDING REFLECTIVE PRACTICE

As we illustrated in Figure 3.1, the coaching process is organized around a cycle of reflective practice, a cycle which continuously flows from goal setting to action to reflection. Feedback, then, is the fuel of reflective practice. The goal of the coaching process is to develop self-actualized educators who are always engaged in this cycle. Coaches support the development of reflective practice through relationship, listening, observing, questioning, and by providing feedback.

In Part II of this book, we will explore the deeper strategies that a coach can bring to the coaching relationship, and we will apply these strategies to real issues we have confronted in our coaching practice.

PART II

Blended Coaching Strategies

In Part I of this book, we shared our general definition of coaching and outlined our case for coaching as an essential tool for the professional development of school leaders. We also reviewed the basic skills that effective coaches bring to their practice.

In Part II, we explore the fundamental structure of coaching conversations and relationships—what we call coaching strategies. We suggest that effective leadership coaches draw upon a variety of coaching strategies and move fluidly between them through a process we call Blended Coaching. We suggest that there are two basic approaches to coaching: instructional coaching and facilitative coaching. Within and between those broad categories, we discuss consultative, collaborative, and transformational approaches. Finally, we suggest that the goal of our work has to be systems change that has a lasting and positive impact upon students.

CHAPTER 6

What Is Blended Coaching?

> *Though this be madness, yet there is method in't.*
> —William Shakespeare

> *I have yet to see any problem, however complicated, which, when you looked at it in the right way, did not become still more complicated.*
> —Poul Anderson

> *Coaching isn't all fun and games. Sometimes, no matter how nice a guy you are, you are going to have to be an asshole. You can't be a coach if you need to be liked.*
> —Phil Jackson

Coaching is a complex practice, and we are convinced there is no single "right" way to approach it. We do not claim to own any unique or exclusive set of ideas around coaching. We have identified the basic skills we believe to be essential to successful professional coaching: relationship building, listening, observing, questioning, and providing feedback. Effective coaches use a variety of strategies as they apply these generic skills. They draw upon a number of approaches, moving quickly and flexibly through them as required during the course of their coaching sessions.

We arrived at the Blended Coaching model through a variety of experiences, including many years of coaching teachers, principals, and others, as well as training in cognitive coaching, ontological coaching, life coaching, and peer coaching. Because formal professional coaching is a relatively new field, research about it is ongoing. Our own research and that of related fields, however, appear to validate Blended Coaching Strategies as a way of thinking about the coaching process.

If we have made a unique contribution to the practice of professional coaching, it is in acknowledging that effective coaches apply and meld a variety of strategies. We suggest that most, if not all, coaching can be discussed within the context of Blended Coaching strategies and that this framework is helpful in planning, implementing, and evaluating professional coaching.

As prospective coaches work to master the strategies we introduce here, they might also choose to study and practice other approaches. We hope the literature included in the References section of this book will provide a springboard for readers into the many other available sources of useful information about leadership coaching strategies.

WAYS OF DOING, WAYS OF BEING

The learning we experience as human beings involves changing both how we do things (our external behaviors) and who we are (our internal selves). Our actions and our internal processes are inextricably linked, each shaping the other. Think about learning to drive. Initially, you learned *how* to steer, to accelerate, to apply the brakes, to look to the right and the left before making a turn. You were highly cautious and perhaps nervous when you took even a short drive in your own neighborhood. Over time and with practice, the behaviors essential to driving successfully became almost automatic. You internalized them, found yourself comfortable with the process, and *became* a driver.

Jack wants to build a strong team with his two assistant principals at Highline High. He says he is committed to sharing leadership with them and to building their capacity as future principals. For the first time in his career as a principal, with the encouragement and support of his coach, he is meeting weekly with his Assistant Principals (APs) to talk about "big picture" issues. Working in concert with them, he has organized a plan for rotating responsibilities that will allow each AP to take on new and expanded instructional leadership roles. In addition, Jack is examining his own habits of holding power and problems close to his vest and expecting his APs to somehow magically anticipate and unquestioningly comply with his vision and desires.

In order to build a capable leadership team at his site, Jack is changing both *what he does* (by building new structures for communication and shared leadership) and *who he is* (by learning to relax his need for command and control).

Coaches must be prepared to support their coachees in learning to do new things—and old things in new ways. They must also be prepared to support their coachees in learning new ways of being—and changing old ways of being. When we change what we do, we change who we are, and vice versa. A particular coaching interaction may center on either side of this dynamic, and this will influence the coach's choice of strategy.

Learning on one side of the equation will impact the other. For example, it would not be unusual for a coach to assist a site leader to prepare for a parent advisory meeting by helping the leader to clarify the goals for the meeting, develop an agenda, and review mechanisms for increasing attendance. The coach is helping the leader with managerial steps, the things a leader *does*, that are prerequisite to involving parents in decision-making. The coach might then attend and observe the meeting, watching for the ways in which the leader communicates with parents and responds to concerns and suggestions. In sharing feedback with the coachee, the coach offers the opportunity to reflect upon the coachee's interactions and to learn new ways of being with parents.

Because a coach must be able to help the coachee learn both new ways of doing and new ways of being, we suggest coaches be prepared to apply two fundamental strategies: *instructional coaching* and *facilitative coaching*.

Table 6.1 offers a few examples of related *ways of doing* and *ways of being*.

TABLE 6.1 • Ways of Doing and Being

WAYS OF DOING	WAYS OF BEING
Planning an agenda for a parent advisory meeting.	Embracing and utilizing parent involvement and voice.
Building a weekly time schedule to maximize classroom observation time.	Examining all decisions through the lens of impact upon instruction.
Providing teachers with student achievement data.	Building and facilitating a learning community focused on student achievement.
Meeting timelines and following procedures in evaluating staff.	Using the supervision process to uphold high standards and to support ongoing professional growth.

DISPOSITIONS AND WAYS OF BEING

Tony has been a principal at Sirrine Elementary School for three years. He has hired 50% of the teachers in the school and has a good relationship with the support staff. He has made difficult decisions since coming to the school related to teacher assignments, scheduling, academic focus, and school culture. During the monthly meeting with his school leadership team, teachers expressed their concerns regarding the lack of parental and caregiver support for school events. When Tony asked for examples and clarification, Mrs. Simons, the 5th grade lead teacher, shared data she had been collecting from teachers on her team. The data showed that only 26% of English Second Language students' parents were attending parent–teacher conferences and only 15% attended family night. That evening Tony called his coach and shared the information. His coach asked him a direct question: "How do you explain this lack of participation by Latinx families?" Tony's immediate response was "I am concerned that we have not created a school environment where all families feel welcome. I want them to be engaged in a way that they find the experience meaningful and beneficial to themselves and the academic and well-being of their children. I need to work on a plan with my teachers and support staff to better engage all families and the community in decision making opportunities at the school and encourage their involvement and participation."

Tony cares about his students and their families. Teachers have observed him advocate for resources for students and their families. They expect that he will demonstrate what Helm (2010) has identified as five crucial dispositions for school leaders: courage, integrity, caring, strong work ethic, and the ability to think critically. What Helm calls dispositions fall clearly into what we characterize as *ways of being*.

Taylor and Wasicsko (2000) define disposition as the personal qualities or characteristics such as interests, values, beliefs, attitudes, and modes of adjustments that are possessed by individuals. Borko, Liston, and Whitcomb (2007) take the definition a step further suggesting dispositions are connected to actions. They describe dispositions as a person's tendencies to act in a given manner reflecting their beliefs and values. PSEL Standard 8 Meaningful Engagement of Families and Community focuses on the ways in which *an effective educational leader engages families and the community in meaningful, reciprocal, and mutually beneficial ways to promote each student's academic success and well-being*. In Table 6.2 are three examples of criteria for PSEL Standard 8. The criteria suggest an action or

TABLE 6.2 • Meaningful Engagement of Families and Community

PSEL STANDARD 8 CRITERIA	DISPOSITION
Effective Leaders a. Are approachable, accessible, and welcoming to families and members of the community.	• Partnering with families, staff, and communities to ensure fair treatment and equal access to opportunities.
b. Create and sustain positive, collaborative, and productive relationships with families and the community for the benefit of students.	• Using language that promotes a belief in the ability of each student and adult to achieve, particularly those from groups that have been historically marginalized. • Openly valuing the diversity of all members of our community. • Clearly demonstrating that you believe in eliminating inequities and providing each student with what they need to be successful.
c. Engage in regular and open two-way communication with families and the community about the school, students, needs, problems, and accomplishments.	• Paying close attention to which voices aren't being heard and invite them to express their perspective.

behaviors a school leader could take to develop meaningful relationships of families and community coming from an equity-centered dispositions (Leadership Academy, 2020). Dispositions, ways of being, are critically important objects of Blended Coaching.

INSTRUCTIONAL COACHING AND FACILITATIVE COACHING

Sometimes it is appropriate for a coach to teach, to use didactic methods in order to help a coachee to achieve a goal. Coaches typically use *instructional* strategies when they are focusing on a coachee's *way of doing*. For example, to help a coachee get into classrooms more often, a coach might provide an article on time management and work with the coachee to set up new office systems. The coach might shadow the coachee and suggest concrete changes in behavior and process that would make it possible for the coachee to protect the time set aside for classroom observations. Each of these instructional steps would help the principal do a better job of getting into classrooms.

Over time, we change who we are by changing what we do. However, instructional strategies have limitations. They may encourage dependence rather than independence. They teach specific knowledge and skills but fall short when it comes to building fundamental capacity. Coaches can help coachees internalize learning and be transformed by it through *facilitative* strategies, strategies that are constructivist in nature. These support the coachee in learning new *ways of being* through observation, reflection, analysis, reinterpretation, and experimentation.

Let's examine the distinction between these two fundamental coaching strategies as they might apply to Jack, the principal in our earlier example who is committed to building a strong leadership team at Highline High. We will assume that Jack has approached his coach for assistance. Jack's coach might use instructional strategies to help him set up management and governance structures. The coach might share his own experience, provide informative articles, and arrange visits with Jack to other high school sites. To help Jack learn to empower others, however, his coach would take a facilitative approach. This might include observing Jack as he interacts with his assistant principals and providing feedback, asking Jack to reflect on his observed behavior relative to his goals. Jack's coach might ask him to examine his deep assumptions about power, control, and responsibility. His coach might also ask him to role-play conversations with the APs, to try out new ways of operating, and then to step back and evaluate them.

THE MÖBIUS STRIP

Effective coaches move between instructional and facilitative domains as they strive to address coachee needs and accelerate coachee effectiveness. We represent the fluidity of this process by portraying it in the form of a Möbius strip. As we illustrate in Figure 6.1, Blended Coaching Strategies do not occur along a continuum but rather in a dynamic process.

FIGURE 6.1 ● Blended Coaching Strategies as Möbius Strip

SOME CAVEATS

Most coaches find Blended Coaching Strategies to be a comfortable and rational way of envisioning the coaching process. But mastering this approach demands discipline and practice, as coaches must learn to move effectively between facilitative and instructional strategies.

Many educators have been trained in *cognitive coaching*. In its early days, cognitive coaching training and literature left many practitioners believing that it was taboo for a coach to do anything other than to provide objective feedback and to ask reflective questions. Cognitive coaches true to the dogma were limited to the use of facilitative approaches. In our experience, coaches trained in cognitive coaching often have very strong facilitative coaching skills, but struggle with a tension between the vision of coaching they have been taught—"Cognitive Coaching is a non-judgmental process of mediation" (Costa & Garmston, 2002, p. 29). Cognitive coaching acknowledges the consultative and collaborative functions but suggests that "each function plays a significantly different role, with very different mechanisms and intentions" (Costa & Garmston, 2002, p. 9). We have found that in the high-stakes environment of professional education, coaches need to be able to draw upon a broad repertoire of strategies, including instructional strategies, in the course of any coaching conversation. Thus, our model builds upon the outstanding work of Costa and Garmston and others in articulating a constructivist approach to coaching, while integrating other more didactic strategies.

Some coachees do not possess the internal capacity to develop new knowledge and understandings through facilitative coaching. In these cases, it is simply more efficient and effective to share information, advice, and opinions using an instructional approach. But this should not be taken to mean we advocate coaching as "telling." Sitting down with a coachee and sharing stories from the field—"this is what happened to me... this is what I did.... this is what you should do..."—is decidedly *not* a coaching strategy we endorse.

Facilitative strategies have the potential to produce powerful personal growth, and instructional strategies support the development of the knowledge and skills required for success on the job. Coaches must cultivate the ability to recognize, on the spot, which approach is likely to be most effective, and to move easily from one to the other as the situation demands.

In Figure 6.2, we highlight a sequence of selected coaching interventions as Mara supports John, a high school principal, in leading improvements in algebra instruction at Ringwood, a large comprehensive high school.

1. Using a *facilitative* approach, Mara helps John to clarify his concerns and goals in relation to algebra instruction. She also uses facilitative coaching to help him identify teacher leaders and the communication processes he'll use to involve the faculty and parent community.

2. In *instructional* mode, Mara identifies a number of potential sources of student data that should be useful to John, and shows him how to interpret the data. She also provides John with templates of department meeting agendas that other schools use to plan and monitor program improvements.

3. In the *instructional consultative* role, Mara researches potential model programs for Ringwood, recommends that he visit a school with a model program, and recommends employing a consultant to assist the math department leadership team.

4. In the *facilitative* role, Mara leads John through the process of identifying potential barriers to the implementation of an improvement plan.

5. John and Mara visit math classrooms at Ringwood, and Mara uses *facilitative* questioning to help John to ground his assessments of the instructional practices observed and to outline next steps. She uses *instructional* coaching as she shares ideas for schoolwide professional development strategies with John.

FIGURE 6.2 ● The Blended Coaching Dance

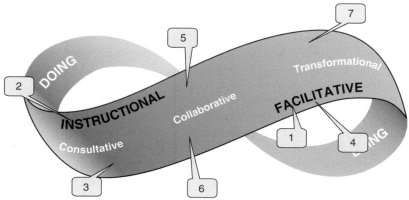

6. Mara is both *instructional* and *facilitative* as she and John *collaborate* in finalizing the plan for algebra program improvement that will be taken to the Curriculum Council for approval.

7. Mara leads John through a *facilitative, transformational* coaching role play to prepare him for difficult conversations with the few parents and teachers who oppose the changes.

8. Back where they started in the blended coaching dance, Mara takes a *facilitative* approach in leading a conversation in which John reflects upon how those difficult conversations went, upon progress to date, and upon possible next steps.

In the chapters that follow, we explore Blended Coaching Strategies in more depth, and we examine the ways in which effective coaches and coachees dance their way around the Möbius strip.

Reflection: How does this model map against other coaching models you are familiar with and/or that you have experienced?

CHAPTER 7

Facilitative Coaching

Facilitative coaching builds upon a coachee's existing skills, knowledge, interpretations, and beliefs—and helps the coachee construct new skills, knowledge, interpretations, and beliefs that will form the basis for future actions. The coach does not focus on sharing professional expert knowledge. Rather, he or she uses facilitative methods to support the coachee in developing the capacity to build expertise through self-actualized reflective practice. In facilitative coaching the locus of control leans toward the coachee. A facilitative coach does not make his or her own assessments and narratives the center of the conversation but leads the coachee to form and examine his or her own assessments and narratives. The coach helps the coachee to gather and interpret data and feedback, develop his or her own perspectives, and analyze and select courses of action.

OUTCOMES OF FACILITATIVE COACHING

Facilitative coaching strategies can have a number of positive outcomes:

Creating New Possibilities by Taking a Fresh Look at Assessments and Narratives. Our assessments and narratives shape our future behaviors and define the possibilities we allow for ourselves. Educators certainly know this; the impact of teacher expectations on student achievement, for example, is very well documented. Let's listen to Principal Williams:

> I give up. It's no use even trying to get Mr. Jones to help his students be more successful. I've talked to him. I've sent

him to workshops. I arranged for him to visit a model classroom. He says the kids are too lazy. The bottom line is, he's lazy. He doesn't want any extra work. He wants to take the easy way out every time.

In this case, Mrs. Williams is assessing Mr. Jones' resistance to change as a case of laziness. While there might be some truth in this, we could probably find plenty of evidence—stated in the form of assertions—that this teacher, who works without breaks with 33 fifth graders five days a week, is not lazy by most standards. Mr. Jones' behavior could be assessed and interpreted in a number of ways. By dismissing Mr. Jones as lazy, this principal is limiting her own ability to support Mr. Jones' professional development.

Her coach might ask how she has supported Mr. Jones, and how her assessment of Mr. Jones as lazy might have influenced his receptivity to her supervision. Might she have inadvertently communicated her assessment to Mr. Jones? How might her assessment of him as a lazy man express low expectations and thus limit the likelihood that he will change his behaviors? What other assessments might be considered that could allow for a more productive future? For example, if it is insecurity rather than laziness that keeps Mr. Jones from holding high expectations for himself and for his students, what kind of support might help Mr. Jones to grow as a professional?

A facilitative coach intervenes by helping a coachee reexamine existing data, gather and evaluate new data, and explore unquestioned assessments. Through this process, which involves questioning, spotlighting data, and providing feedback, the coach challenges the coachee to refine her thinking and develop new narratives and possibilities for action.

Developing Problem-Solving Skills. Through facilitative questions, the coach helps the coachee define and evaluate problems and solutions. The coaching conversation also models the problem-solving language and process that school leaders can use with groups they lead. Looking at a problem from various angles before reaching a conclusion or solution is a skill that supports problem-solving and decision-making. The coach can ask, "How might you get more information about this teacher's skills and knowledge? How could we help this teacher take the first steps toward improvement? How can we build on the teacher's strengths to help him move forward?" The coaching session can end with a plan of action that includes next steps and a plan for evaluating their impact. The coachee moves from being stuck with a no-win assessment to a renewed sense of empowerment and a clear action plan.

Building Self-Reflective Practice. A fundamental goal of facilitative coaching is building the *habits of mind* that constitute reflective practice. A facilitative coach mediates the process of acquiring these habits. Conversations between coach and coachee serve as a model for the internal dialogues of a self-reflective practitioner. This makes it possible for the coachee to challenge her own assessments, perceptions, ideas, narratives, and actions. A self-reflective practitioner attempts to understand events and situations, including how she is perceived by others, from multiple perspectives. She has internalized the plan-act-reflect cycle at the micro and macro levels.

Shifting the Locus of Control From Coach to Coachee. Linked to the goal of building self-reflective practice in the coachee is the long-term goal of shifting the locus of control in the coaching relationship from the coach to the coachee. As novices, we don't know what we don't know, and we rely on our coaches to help us identify our needs and next steps. As we gain experience, we still benefit from the discipline and outside perspective that comes with coaching, while at the same time we have the internal resources to guide our own professional growth.

APPLYING FACILITATIVE STRATEGIES

As we discuss Chapter 3, an effective coaching relationship is grounded in trust. This is particularly true in facilitative coaching, as we probe our coachee with questions. And, before launching into a facilitative approach, the coach must determine whether the issues at hand hold the promise of important learning when balanced against constraints posed by time. Facilitative coaching is often time consuming and indirect, and is not appropriate for every situation. Facilitative coaching may not be the best approach to helping a coachee deal with an urgent or low stakes operational issue.

A coach is not in a position to help a coachee work through every single problem as soon as it presents itself. Instead, there should be a triage process in place to determine which issues are to be acknowledged and set aside, which are to be tackled quickly and directly, and which are best addressed through facilitative processes over time. These include the deeper issues that promise big payoffs. This process can be informed by tools such as 360° survey instruments, self-assessments, and goals statements developed for internal or external evaluators.

A reflective conversation in which the coach maintains a facilitative stance may not be the most efficient way to share information, but it is a powerful means of developing internal capacity. Successful facilitative coaching rests upon the assumption that the coachee possesses or can independently acquire the skills, knowledge, and dispositions required to resolve a question or need. A reflective conversation about rewriting the school plan will not go far if the novice has little knowledge or experience in relation to the mechanics and regulatory aspects of the school planning process.

On the other hand, let's suppose the coachee grasps the technical requirements she must meet in rewriting the plan. What she may not understand is that a school plan can be a tool for school improvement. She is looking at the plan revision simply as a project she will complete—without significant input—to bring her school into compliance. The coach, however, can facilitate a conversation that leads the coachee to see the plan as a lever for genuine change. The coach sees that using a facilitative approach will help the principal grasp the connection between revising the plan, improving the school, and effective leadership.

PRINCIPAL: Maybe you could help me get my plan revision done. You could read my draft.

COACH: Sure. Tell me what you are trying to accomplish here.

PRINCIPAL: Well, it's an update I have to turn in to the district and the State Department of Education. The teachers are busy with the new mathematics adoption and report cards.

COACH: Sounds like you want to rewrite the plan yourself and shelter your teachers from the work.

PRINCIPAL: That's where I am headed, my staff is feeling pretty stressed as it is.

COACH: I am wondering what your priority is here— getting the plan done without creating stress for your staff, or using the plan as a tool for moving your school.

PRINCIPAL: That's worth thinking about. I guess I would like to get folks' input and buy-in. How can I do that without putting too much onto my staff?

COACH: Great question! Let's think about what a more inclusive process would look like.

BASIC MOVES OF FACILITATIVE COACHING

Facilitative coaching is a deceptively simple process that leads a coachee through a reflective conversation by questioning, paraphrasing, and summarizing. Table 7.1 outlines five basic moves in facilitative coaching and provides sample language stems for each.

TABLE 7.1 • Five Moves in Facilitative Coaching

Opening	"What do we hope to achieve in our meeting today?"
	"In following up on last week, this is what we agreed to work on ..."
	"Tell me about your progress in relation to ..."
Paraphrasing	"You are noticing that ..."
	"In other words ..."
	"You're saying that ..."
Clarifying Questions	"To what extent ...?"
	"It would help me if you would give me an example."
	"Tell me more about ..."
	"Tell me what you mean when you ..."
Paraphrasing With Interpretation	"What you are describing could mean ..."
	"Based on what you have described so far ..."
	"Tell me if what you are saying means that ..."
Mediational Questions	"What's another way you might ...?"
	"What would it look like if ...?"
	"How might she react if ...?"
	"What might be his rationale for ...?"
	"What might be an argument against ...?"
Summarizing Statements	"Let's review the key points of the discussion ..."
	"Can you describe your next steps?"
	"We'll know that you have achieved your goals when ..."

Source: Adapted from Gilley and Broughton (1996, pp. 136–141).

OPENING

Any coaching meeting should begin with an opening. Opening dialogues are a sort of agenda setting, establishing the special space that is a coaching conversation. It is a time to set the goals and expectations for the meeting. It can also be a time to maintain personal connections, and to agree to discuss "problems de jour" for some portion of the session.

COACH: Are there any particular issues or concerns you want to kick around today before we continue our work around your literacy initiative? At our last meeting we agreed that you would share your plan for the grade level PLC meetings. We have about an hour before we are going to get into classrooms.

PARAPHRASING

In paraphrasing, the coach restates the speaker's message— "Let me see if I understand"—to test his own understanding and the speaker's clarity. When the speaker hears his own message restated by the listener, the speaker has the opportunity to evaluate it and become aware of how it is being heard.

PRINCIPAL: So we had our first meeting to brainstorm strategies to improve our literacy program. Things went well. We got a lot done. The seventh-grade team was off-task, but the rest of them were great.

COACH: So, you were pleased with the outcomes of the meeting but have a concern about the participation of the seventh-grade team.

As simple as it may seem, paraphrasing is a powerful technique. It forces the speaker out of his own head. We tend to speak in generalities that reveal unrefined thinking. When we hear our language reflected back to us by a listener, we are stimulated to fine-tune our thinking as well as our speaking.

CLARIFYING QUESTIONS

Clarifying questions are essential to facilitative coaching for several reasons. First, they are key to the process of identifying the needs of the coachee and the nature of the issues at hand. The coach can use them to lead the coachee through a process of discovery as the coachee is asked to think more precisely and deeply about a given issue.

Clarifying questions also forestall the tendency to move directly and perhaps too hastily to a solution, as they offer the coachee the opportunity to think for more than a few seconds about any one topic. They also extend the coach's opportunity to listen to the coachee's language and uncover underlying issues, feelings, and attitudes. When the coach asks, "Can you explain what you mean by…," the coachee will restate or revise his words and be more likely to reveal his attitudes and beliefs as a result.

Clarifying questions can also lead coachees to find connections between ideas as well as to develop and maintain focus. In response to "What is important about…," it is not unusual for a coachee to answer with "Now that I've thought about…," and shift his perspective on the issue.

PRINCIPAL: The seventh-grade team is just always a step behind everyone else.

COACH: Can you give me a few examples of this?

Clarifying questions help coachees gather and interpret data and are powerful tools for pushing them to examine their assessments. Asking, "How do you know that?" or, "What evidence do you have to support that judgment?" moves the coachee away from unspoken assumptions and brings ideas to the surface so they can be examined more readily. Spending enough time paraphrasing and asking clarifying questions are essential steps to take before moving more deeply into facilitative coaching or deciding to shift to instructional coaching.

PARAPHRASING WITH INTERPRETATION

In paraphrasing with interpretation, a coach goes beyond restating his understanding of a coachee's utterance. He inserts his own perspective and tests ideas or interpretations with the coachee. By bringing a different lens, background knowledge, and experiences to the conversation, the coach can assist the coachee by offering new ways to represent herself and her concerns.

PRINCIPAL: Let's see. There's the body language. They give each other looks and do some eye rolling when certain suggestions are made. Then they have inside jokes and laugh about things that the rest of us don't know about. Then they usually bring papers to grade during the meetings so they aren't really attentive to what's going on.

COACH:	Sounds like there are patterns of behavior that have been established within their small group that sidetrack your process and that they feel free to exhibit in the larger group.

MEDIATIONAL QUESTIONS

Mediational questions are crafted in order to produce a shift in thinking. Costa and Garmston (2002) describe a "mediator" as one who comes between another person and a *task* or between another person and *meaning*. The mediator—for our purposes, the coach—influences the direction and flow of another person's thinking through conversation. The coach listens for what the coachee understands and articulates—but with an ear tuned for what the coachee *isn't* saying. Sometimes coachees aren't forthright because they are unwilling to expose vulnerabilities. At other times, coachees tell it as they see it but are limited by their own experiences and perspective.

By exploring past actions using a question such as "What would it have looked like if... ?," the coach can help the coachee analyze what worked or didn't work and compare and contrast what was planned with what ensued. By posing future-oriented questions—"What would it look like if...?" or "What's another way you might... ?"—the coach can guide the thinking of the coachee in new directions into unexplored territory, and the coachee can generate or imagine new possibilities. By asking, "How would...be different from...?," the coach pushes the coachee to compare and contrast ideas, which helps the coachee understand a situation from various points of view. Through mediational questioning, the coach encourages the development of the coachee's problem analysis skills. Being able and willing to analyze a situation thoroughly before moving into action is an essential skill for school leaders and one of the central skills developed through the coaching process.

PRINCIPAL:	Yes. This goes on at every meeting. We wrote out meeting norms at the beginning of the year—but that didn't help much.
COACH:	What would it look like if you were to build those norms into your culture?
PRINCIPAL:	Well, as I said, they're posted—but we haven't really discussed them since we posted them. I think I need to bring them up at the beginning of each meeting. Or maybe what we need to do is

reexamine them and decide how well they're working. This would get the teachers to point out how we could do better, and that would help everyone recommit to the norms.

COACH: It sounds to me like your narrative, or explanation of this, is one of plain old bad behavior on the part of the seventh-grade team. Might there be a deeper explanation for their behavior? Is there a lack of capacity on the part of some members of the team or a belief that they should not be responsible for literacy instruction?

SUMMARIZING STATEMENTS

Coaching conversations can include many digressions, but they should be focused and goal oriented and progress smoothly from exploration to interpretation to commitment to action. Summarizing statements sustain this trajectory. Noting the key points, insights, or possible next steps, the coach can periodically bring these forward with summarizing statements such as "It sounds like you now think that..." or "Here's what we've covered so far...." These statements allow the coachee to consider, revise, and refine what's been said. By sorting the key ideas from a lengthy conversation, the coach helps the coachee organize thoughts so they can more easily be analyzed and evaluated. Summarizing questions—"Can you describe your next steps?"—encourage the coachee to master this mental process of sorting and prioritizing. Thus, summarizing helps the coachee maintain focus and clarity, pinpoint next steps, and review commitments.

COACH: Well, in the past several minutes you've mentioned a few things. Let's write down those you can commit to as action steps.

PRINCIPAL: OK. I'm going to put a discussion of the norms on the next meeting agenda with the goal of recommitting or modifying them if necessary. Then for the rest of the year, I'll start each meeting by reviewing them. I wonder what else we could do to make it work.

COACH: And how are you going to get a handle on the possible deeper causes of the seventh grade team's lack of focus?

PRINCIPAL: I'm going to get into their classrooms and am going to have individual conversations with each team member.

COACH: OK, I'm going to put these commitments into my notes and we'll talk about what you have learned when we meet the week after next.

You can see how the facilitative conversation shifts as the coach and the coachee identify areas that need clarification or exploration. Once a few action steps are determined, it can still be useful to refine them by posing additional clarifying and mediational questions. This may create even more possibilities for action. The coach might ask, "How do you think the faculty will respond to revisiting the norms? What indications do you have that the group would support active implementation of positive meeting norms? How do you think you could involve some teacher leaders in this process?" The coach supports the principal's success by listening carefully, asking probing questions, and encouraging the coachee to reflect, ground assessments, explore new possibilities, and commit to productive next steps.

What might have happened in our vignette if this principal had been unfamiliar with processes for using meeting norms? What if our principal were unfamiliar with processes for coming to consensus? What does a coach do when the conversation stops because the principal lacks the necessary knowledge or skills to move forward? To support principals in building their knowledge and skills, coaches must be prepared to use instructional strategies.

Reflection: Think about and write down a problem or dilemma you are currently facing in your own personal or professional life. Next, write a series of facilitative questions you would ask yourself if you were your coach.

CHAPTER 8

Instructional Coaching

From studies of learning in and out of school, it appears that people build up knowledge by solving real problems using available clues, tools and social supports. Traditional apprenticeships provide one model of this kind of learning. In an apprenticeship, a beginner develops flexible skills and conditional knowledge by working on genuine tasks in the company of a master. Take, for example, the situated and sequenced process by which apprentice tailors learn to produce garments. From observing masters, apprentices develop an image of how an entire garment is produced while they work on specific components (e.g., a sleeve) and practice specific skills (e.g., cutting, pressing, using the sewing machine). In such an apprenticeship, knowing cannot be separated from doing.

—Sharon Feiman-Nemser and Janine Remillard,
authors of Perspectives on Learning to Teach

Coaches have to be prepared to teach, to share their expertise and professional resources with their coachees. When a coachee has the requisite knowledge and skills, we often use facilitative strategies to help the coachee deepen understandings and think through options for action. However, there are times when a more direct approach is appropriate. In these cases the coach must take on an instructional role.

Instructional coaching is an approach in which the coach shares his or her own experience, expertise, and craft wisdom with the coachee by using traditional teaching strategies. These may include modeling, providing resources, direct instruction, and even advice giving. The intended outcomes remain the same: to support the coachee in clarifying and committing to appropriate goals and in taking effective action. In the Blended

Coaching model, instructional coaching is usually nested in facilitative coaching as coaches work with coachees to assess needs and as coachees develop understandings and start to apply what they know.

As we have noted, education professions demand the mastery of a multitude of skills and areas of knowledge. School leaders in particular are often expected to know it all and to know it now. An effective coach can make a significant difference in the success of principals and other educators, particularly novices, by providing them with "just in time" instructional coaching.

APPLICATIONS OF INSTRUCTIONAL COACHING

Time is almost always of the essence in the day-to-day lives of educators. When it is clear that the coachee does not possess the knowledge or internal resources required for action, and when that action must be taken quickly, instructional coaching is often the most effective strategy. Sometimes a coachee's needs are simple and operational. For example, a principal may need to know regulations for counting instructional minutes and how to use a template to keep track of them. At other times the needs might be more complex. A principal with no background in bilingual education may need to evaluate several bilingual teachers. In both cases, the principal can immediately benefit from professional knowledge, resources, or advice provided by the coach.

Reflection: Why would instructional coaching, guided by facilitative questioning, be the right move in the following situation?

COACH:	How is your planning coming for your opening staff meeting?
COACHEE:	Pretty well. One thing I want to do is review our spring test data.
COACH:	How will you go about this? What do you want to accomplish?
COACHEE:	I'm not sure. First off, I've got binders full of printouts, but I am not sure how to interpret or present the results. Also, I want to do more than just pass out numbers, but I am not sure just how to proceed.

BACKGROUND KNOWLEDGE AND PROCESS SKILLS

School leaders must be able to perform fairly simple and clear-cut tasks such as filling out forms and following timelines. They are also responsible for highly sophisticated tasks such as meeting facilitation and instructional coaching. Completing them requires both background knowledge and process skills.

Background knowledge is what one must know, and process skills are what one must be able to do. In order to provide leadership in implementing the special education IEP process at her site, a principal should possess knowledge about special education law and programs, and process skills for facilitating meetings, problem-solving, and conflict resolution. Unpacking the knowledge and skills required to accomplish a task or goal is a way of focusing the coaching process (just as it is when planning instruction in a K-12 classroom). Table 8.1 provides an analysis of the knowledge and skills the school leader needs to design a meeting in which the faculty analyze survey data. The table identifies background knowledge and process skills the coach and coachee need to know and be able to analyze survey data. This model can be adapted based on the knowledge and skills that will be needed for the problem of practice being discussed during a coaching session.

TABLE 8.1 • Completed Analysis of Knowledge and Skills Template

In order to DESIGN A MEETING in which the faculty analyzes survey data

• A school leader must know (Background knowledge)
   ✔ Elements of effective meetings
   ✔ Small and large group discussion processes
   ✔ Meeting norms
   ✔ Elements of effective surveys
   ✔ Background about the school/community relationships
   ✔ Background about previous use of surveys at this school
 	
 • A school leader must know how to (Process skills)
   ✔ Design and communicate the agenda
   ✔ Share leadership
   ✔ Encourage positive norms
   ✔ Facilitate meetings
   ✔ Facilitate interpretation of data
   ✔ Facilitate discussion and decision-making

Exercise: Use the template in Table 8.2 to practice analyzing the background knowledge and the process skills needed to complete the following tasks:

- Lead the revision of the school plan
- Hire a new language arts teacher
- Set up the master schedule (secondary) or class configurations (elementary)
- Supervise and evaluate a teacher
- Analyze assessment data

TABLE 8.2 • Sample Analysis of Knowledge and Skills Template

*In order to*_____
• My coachee must know (Background knowledge) ✔ _____ ✔ _____ ✔ _____ ✔ _____ ✔ _____ ✔ _____ • My coachee must know how to (Process skills) ✔ _____ ✔ _____ ✔ _____ ✔ _____ ✔ _____ ✔ _____

AVOIDING "WAR STORIES"

A coach can offer personal thoughts and experiences that support, reassure, and motivate the coachee. However, coaches must resist the temptation to turn coaching into the sharing of "war stories." There is no evidence to suggest that hearing the travails and triumphs of a veteran will help another administrator move forward with his own situation. Coaches should remember that adults will resist anything they see as an attack on their competence. Storytelling and advice giving can put coachees on the defensive if they come to the conclusion that the coach's situation is different from their own; if they believe the coach does not understand their unique situation; or if they interpret the coach's success story as conveying superiority. A good example is when the coach has no experience leading a school through a pandemic and the principal is still leading the school in a COVID environment and believes the coach doesn't understand what he has been dealing with. Often the principal will express frustration with the coach and say, "you don't understand the problems I have to deal with such as not enough substitutes, mask mandates, testing students and staff every day, and organizing virtual learning opportunities for students." Rather than providing a war story about when the coach led a school following a tornado, or wildfire, or flooding, the coach should use this as an opportunity to listen and learn more about the school environment in which the coachee is working and avoid examples that may further alienate the teacher and harm the coaching relationship. Demonstrating empathy and support is more important than spending an hour telling the principal how you handled a problem. This does not mean that the ideas you have are not worthy of sharing. We are saying be cautious in using these "war stories" unless they are good examples and can be replicated.

GETTING PERMISSION TO INSTRUCT

Even novice school leaders are often expected to be experts by their subordinates. Principals are very aware that they must appear both knowledgeable and competent. Though a highly trained, responsible educator, the principal may feel insecure about new challenges and may be reluctant to admit any lack of knowledge or skills: "I was an English teacher and program coordinator. If I admit I really don't know much about mathematics programs, what will the folks in the math department think?" To ensure that the coachee is comfortable with the role of "learner," the coach asks for consent before moving into in-depth instructional coaching. This can be done simply by asking questions such as:

- Would you like more information about...?
- Would you like to spend some time looking at...?
- Would you like me to describe some options for you?

PRINCIPAL: So I'm doing my formal observation of my English as a Second Language teacher and when I went in to observe a lesson, she was speaking almost entirely in Spanish. They were talking about the seasons, and she had picture cards and words in English—but they were talking about their experiences in Spanish—so almost the entire lesson was taking place in Spanish.

COACH: Can you describe what you expected to see?

PRINCIPAL: Well, that's where I'm just not sure. I'm not really sure exactly what portion of the lesson should be in Spanish. But it seems like if she is going to teach English, she should be speaking more English.

COACH: *Would it be helpful to review the research* on language acquisition and to look at some model ESL lessons?

PRINCIPAL: Yes! And do you have those in writing so that I could share them with my teachers?

Once the coachee accepts an invitation to learn new information, skills, or tools, the coach can proceed—ever mindful of the need to monitor and adjust based on the coachee's needs and responses.

As an experienced administrator, the coach may know "just what to do" in a particular situation. But he must proceed carefully, using language that keeps the new information, skills, or tools away from his personal experience base and his own ego. Avoid sentence stems such as "I used to…" or "Once, I…" so that the coachee is able to reject a suggestion without putting herself in the position of embarrassing or disagreeing with her coach. Notice how the following sentence stems keep the coach's identity and ego out of the conversation:

- There are a number of approaches that might work.
- There are a number of appropriate strategies.
- Should we investigate how Marge has approached this?
- Most practitioners believe that…
- Some principals have tried … and it might work for you.
- It might be helpful to…
- A couple of things to keep in mind are…
- The research on this suggests that…

Again, useful phrases are italicized below:

PRINCIPAL: You know there have been a lot of comments about our faculty meetings taking too long, so at my faculty meeting for this Thursday, I'm trying out my new style of agenda. We're designating who will lead each item, and we're stating the number of minutes that item can take. I ran it by my leadership team and they think it's a great idea. I'm hoping this new structure can keep the meeting under control.

COACH: Having the number of minutes each item can take is really helpful. *Some principals* also have a timekeeper who gives a one- or two-minute warning when time is almost up.

PRINCIPAL: That's a good idea ... I think that would really work here.

COACH: *Sometimes* that role is shared or *sometimes* there's one person who is particularly good at it and who wants to do it all the time.

PRINCIPAL: Oh, I have someone who would be great at that and I know she'd really like that job. She was one of the most concerned about the meetings lasting too long.

COACH: Have you thought about how you might evaluate the success of this new process?

MOVING BETWEEN INSTRUCTIONAL AND FACILITATIVE COACHING

A typical coaching session shifts fluidly between facilitative and instructional approaches. The coach may move briefly into instructional coaching—to offer new information or point out something the coachee has missed—and then return to facilitative coaching once the coachee has the knowledge that is needed to proceed.

COACH: What's been working well for you?

PRINCIPAL: I got to attend the Learning Forward Conference —and got lots of ideas.

COACH: What ideas are foremost in your thinking right now?

PRINCIPAL: Well, they talked about how important it is to have a two-hour literacy block. So I looked at our bell schedule, and if I move recess by ten minutes, we can do it. Since we don't have a faculty meeting for another two weeks, I thought I'd just go ahead and put it in our Monday bulletin so that we can get started right away—so that's pretty much worked out. I'm excited about having a stronger focus on literacy.

COACH: Can we spend a few minutes thinking about that change in bell schedule and what some of the initial reactions and responses might be when teachers find out about it via a memo?

PRINCIPAL: Uh-oh. Is this one of those land mines?

COACH: It could be! There are a few things to keep in mind as you decide which decisions you'll make by yourself, and which you'll take to the faculty. In general, the more directly a change affects the classroom, the more teachers will want to be part of the discussion and decision.

PRINCIPAL: I suppose I could ruffle some feathers here.

COACH: So let's think about teachers who have been accustomed to planning instruction in certain time blocks for several years. How might they respond if you issue a change in schedule through a memo ... with no discussion?

PRINCIPAL: OK. I get it. I can think of a few teachers already who might get really upset ... let me go get those memos before the teachers see them. Then I'd like to plan out how to approach this change.

COACH: And let's start with your vision for a literacy block. How would you like to see that time used? What would it take to ensure that quality instruction was taking place in every classroom during this chunk of time?

CHAPTER 9

Collaborative Coaching

J anet is a principal who has just returned from a district meeting. She received a packet of information about conducting a self-study for a Compliance Review of state and federal categorical programs. She has the timeline and list of tasks—but is overwhelmed and has no idea how to start, what the process should look like, how she should or shouldn't involve staff, and what the outcome of the self-study should be. She's in the middle of rewriting her school improvement plan and isn't sure how or whether to integrate these processes.

In this scenario, the principal possesses a significant amount of knowledge about the school's categorical programs, and she understands the practical aspects of completing a self-study that meets program requirements. What is difficult for her to sort out is the role that the self-study could play in the larger scheme of her school improvement processes. She would benefit from facilitative coaching as she prioritizes tasks and makes a plan to take advantage of a compliance review process to support moving her school toward the realization of its vision. She will also benefit from her coach's experience in managing large and complex projects that span several months, are data driven, and require the participation of stakeholders.

This scenario presents an opportunity for what we call *collaborative coaching*. This strategy falls between the core strategies of instruction and facilitation because the coach is constantly in both modes working through a project that is collaborative in nature. The coach gets her hands dirty and does at least some portion of the work alongside the coachee. The focus is on concrete action with a larger goal of developing knowledge, skills, and internal capacity that can be generalized to other situations. In the case we have outlined above, Janet and her coach might sit down and jointly develop a plan for conducting the self-study and completing the school plan. The coach might help Janet develop a presentation outlining the school's progress in increasing student achievement. He might also review Janet's self-study and plan documents.

USES OF COLLABORATIVE COACHING

Collaborative coaching is appropriate when the coach and coachee have identified a need or problem conducive to shared work that promises to generate powerful learning for the coachee. This strategy is not about a coach rescuing an overwhelmed coachee by doing the coachee's job. It is applicable when a clear project or task is identified—such as evaluating the effectiveness of a literacy program, planning a specific meeting agenda, writing a difficult letter or evaluation, or setting up budget processes. In these examples, the coach and coachee each possess pieces of what is required to complete the project. Via collaborative coaching, the plan or product developed by the coachee will be better than what would have been achieved working in isolation. In an effective collaborative project, the coach brings expertise, resources, and perspective, while the coachee brings intimate knowledge of the situation and the positional authority to implement actions.

Collaborative coaching is not appropriate if the process would undermine the authority and image of the coachee. The coach must be sensitive to the way the coachee perceives their relationship and responds to coaching. Does the coachee tend to give up power when the coach "takes over"? If this is the case, then it is best to stick to facilitative coaching strategies. But when the coachee feels confident about what she brings to the table and seeks to use the expertise and assistance of the coach to help accomplish clear goals, the collaboration can move forward productively.

AN EXAMPLE OF COLLABORATIVE COACHING

In the following example, the principal and coach recognize the need to revitalize the governance structure at Wisconsin High.

PRINCIPAL: The school board has asked us to review the core reading lists for our English classes and submit a new set of recommendations.

COACH:	Can you give me some background on this issue?
PRINCIPAL:	We've been getting a lot of challenges lately, parents complaining about books like *Catcher in the Rye*, and some undercurrents against some of the modern selections on our lists like *House on Mango Street* and *Beloved*.
COACH:	Tell me how you would like this review process to play out.
PRINCIPAL:	Well, I'd like to be inclusive, but I don't want to open Pandora's box. And I want the professionals to have the final say.
COACH:	What kind of structures does the school have in place for this sort of decision-making?
PRINCIPAL:	Not much. There are the department chairs and department meetings, and on the parent side there are some booster clubs. The previous principal let the parent council die a quiet death, and I don't think that students have ever had a voice in curriculum issues. And I haven't got a clue how to juggle all of these groups.
COACH:	Sounds like you would like to develop a clearer, more inclusive governance structure here, and this reading list issue provides the rationale for you to take this on.
COACHEE:	Absolutely.
COACH:	It might be a good use of our time to put our heads together on this issue. Would you be interested in my help designing a governance model for Wisconsin?

In collaborative coaching, the coach may offer an array of approaches or solutions to the issue being addressed. But the coachee determines the processes and tools that will best match her school. It is critical that the coach not push a particular remedy onto the coachee, but let her articulate the unique needs and select the best solution. It is the principal who will step out alone in front of the stakeholders with the plan or product of collaboration—and the principal must fully own it. In the beginning, the coach might be in the lead, but by the end of the collaboration, the coachee should be firmly holding the reins (Table 9.1).

TABLE 9.1 • Collaborative Coaching Scenario: Governance

	WISCONSIN HIGH	
Step 1	The need is identified by the coachee and clarified through the coaching process.	*The principal wants to bring an inclusive process to an instructional issue, but there is no structure in place. She lacks experience in this area and requests the coach's support.*
Step 2	The coachee sets the outcome and agrees to collaborate.	*The principal articulates her goal and vision with the support of the coach. The coach agrees to work with the principal to develop a governance structure model and to assist the principal in shepherding its implementation.*
Step 3	The coach shares available resources and ideas and poses questions and suggestions.	*The coach shares research and articles on high school governance. He identifies high schools in the region with successful governance models and puts the coachee in touch with the principals of those schools. He arranges a meeting between himself, the principal, and the superintendent to clarify understanding of the district's expectations.*
Step 4	The coachee selects resources, clarifies needs, and accepts/rejects/modifies the options generated in conversation between coach and coachee.	*Together, the principal and coach identify the characteristics of a model that would work best for the school. Together they generate options for a structure that includes parent, staff, and student advisory bodies and outlines suggestions for their respective roles. The coach drafts several organizational charts for the principal to review and to share with others.*
Step 5	The coach and coachee work together to support the implementation of the project.	*The principal agrees to the formation of several advisory groups. The coach and principal draft a task-analysis and timeline for the creation of the structure and for the implementation of the core reading review process.*
Step 6	The coach continues to draw attention to gaps, offer resources, and refine the thinking and decisions of the coachee through listening, observing, questioning, and providing feedback.	*The implementation of the governance structure is the subject of ongoing review over the course of the year. The coach attends several parent advisory meetings for the purpose of providing feedback to the principal.*
Step 7	The coachee makes the final decisions about the product and the process.	*The buck always stops at the principal's desk. The coach leads the principal through a "cycle of inquiry" process around the implementation of the governance model, guiding the principal as she selects next steps.*

Principals and assistant principals are confronted with problems and tasks on a daily basis. Some of the issues can be overwhelming and stressful. A coach can provide the principal or assistant principal with the opportunity to collaborate, which often leads to new knowledge and skills. Being in a school leadership role can be lonely and isolating. Working with the coach who is nonjudgmental and serves as a colleague and supporter of the school leader's success often results in confidence building and the willingness to be more creative when approaching a school problem in a collaborative manner.

Reflection: How can a coach draw a line between serving as a collaborator and taking over ownership of a task or problem? Think of a time when you have participated in a balanced and successful collaboration.

CHAPTER 10

Consultative Coaching

Consultative coaching is a form of instructional coaching that relies upon specific expertise a coach can bring to a coaching relationship. Peter Block defines a consultant as "a person in a position to have some influence over an individual, a group, or an organization, but who has no direct power to make changes or implement programs" (Block, 2000, p. 2). In contrast to collaborative coaching, in the consultative mode a coach shares perspective, knowledge, and advice, but does not own or participate in any action that results from the coaching process.

Consultative coaching typically focuses upon areas of technical knowledge or skill. The coach-as-consultant possesses resources or expertise that will benefit the coachee and her professional practice. In addition to sharing knowledge and resources, the consultative coach might carry out data gathering on behalf of the coachee and may provide specific recommendations in particular situations.

Jessie is concerned because achievement data for his eighth-grade students indicate a discrepancy between their language and math scores. The data show that aggregate scores in language drop during the three years that students spend in Jessie's school, particularly for students of color. In his efforts to figure out what is going on, he has visited the school's English and social studies classrooms many times. He sees well-managed classrooms taught by experienced teachers. He has a few ideas as to what might be happening; he suspects that there is a need for more differentiated instruction, but by and large, he is stumped by the unsatisfactory scores. He asks his coach, a highly successful middle-school principal in a former life, for assistance.

BASIC STEPS IN
CONSULTATIVE COACHING

Determine the Need and Agree Upon a Consultative Approach. In this example, the principal—Jessie—shares his data with the coach and expresses his concerns. Using a facilitative approach, the coach helps Jessie clarify the need. She then tells Jessie that she has some expertise in secondary language arts instruction through content areas, and offers to provide consultative support. Once the two agree that she will serve in a consultant role on this problem, the coach works with Jessie to gather additional data and to deepen her understanding of the situation. In this case, she will conduct classroom observations with Jessie, examine test data, and review performance by teacher, year, and subgroup. Once she has a handle on what's happening in the classroom, she and Jessie can discuss the school's dynamics, the history of instructional programs, and professional development prior to reviewing potential courses of action.

Provide Advice, Examples, and Resources. Once they agree on the need, the coach, as an expert, can provide resources and advice. It is helpful to set aside a specific time for this purpose during which it is made clear that the coach is playing a consultative role. In our example, the coach shares a data analysis that is disaggregated by gender, ethnicity, and quartile. She shares several articles on differentiated instruction in literacy at the secondary level. They discuss options for approaching these issues in light of the school's particular needs. The coach recommends potential action steps to the principal, including conducting an analysis of achievement data with the staff, creating a professional development plan, and establishing accelerated and intervention curricula in newly created student groupings, building in culturally responsive curricula, and focusing upon improving student–teacher relationships.

Extend Support Beyond the One-to-One Coaching Relationship. The consultative coach can support the implementation and evaluation of program improvements in a variety of ways. As long as the role is explicit, short term, and based in the area of the coach's expertise, the consultative coach can engage with staff and others in the consultant role. In this example, the coach agrees to conduct a mini workshop for John and his leadership team on culturally responsive language arts instruction in content areas. She also suggests that the leadership team visit several other schools in the region and arranges those visits.

Conduct a Cycle of Inquiry as a Process for Instructional Decision-Making. Principals are under constant pressure to solve problems and manage situations quickly. The problem with a quick fix is that no time was spent trying to understand the problem in order to address the causative factors that may continue if not resolved. This is particularly true when the problem is instructional. The Cycle of Inquiry is a process that can be used by the coach and coachee to engage in a continual process of instructional improvement and analysis. The steps vary depending on the cycle of inquiry model. For example, the Center for Educational Leadership at the University of Washington (2014) teaches a four-step process (Figure 10.1):

1. Analyze evidence to develop problems of practice

2. Determine an area of focus

3. Implement, plan, and support learning

4. Analyze impact

FIGURE 10.1 ● Cycle of Inquiry for Instructional Decision–Making

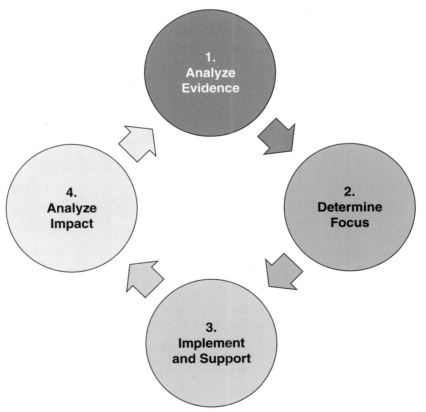

Source: Austin (2015).

Most models begin with the collection and examination of data in order to better understand the problem, identify gaps and trends, generate causative factors, and to initiate change ideas. The second phase is often the testing phase when the principal and his or her team try some of the new ideas and collect additional data. The final step is to examine the data, see if any changes occurred, and either adopt or abandon the new idea or strategy.

THE RISKS OF CONSULTATIVE COACHING

Consultative coaching is an approach to be applied with restraint. Its overuse can build dependency—and *independence* is what coaching is intended to foster. A coach in the consultative role can easily undermine a coachee's confidence and professional growth by being patronizing or prescriptive. Imposing a particular style of leadership or specific practices that aren't chosen by the principal can be disempowering and unproductive. Furthermore, coaches can be wrong in their analysis and recommendations. Coachees may hesitate to challenge the advice because they look up to, and respect, their coaches.

Coaches must also be knowledgeable about and careful to respect established practices and district philosophy. When projects are visible to the school community and the principal doesn't really own them but attributes them instead to the coach, the authority of the principal can be undermined in the eyes of stakeholders. In addition, when problems or conflicts come up, the coach may be targeted for blame by stakeholders and by the principal. Of course, the coach, rather than the coachee, may receive all the credit if things go well. Either way, the coaching relationship as well as the credibility of the principal can be damaged in a way that runs counter to the goals of coaching.

Reflection: What are areas in which you possess the expertise to provide consultative coaching? What are some areas in which you should resist any temptation to provide consultative support?

CHAPTER 11

Transformational Coaching

Succeeding at just about anything is not just about what you know. It is also about who you are. Professional coaches must be prepared to support their coachees in awareness of and growth in their *ways of being* as well as their acquisition of new knowledge and skills. This is why the right side of our Möbius strip includes an approach to facilitative coaching that we refer to as *transformational coaching*.

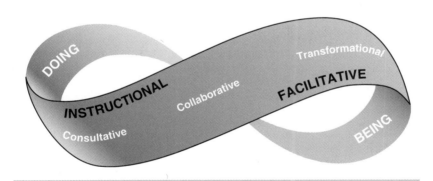

We have discussed the critical importance of interpersonal and communication skills, cultural proficiency, and emotional intelligence for education professionals. While there are cognitive dimensions to each of these performance areas, they must also be addressed in terms of the deeper and more change-resistant domains of disposition and personality, the internal inclinations that constitute our ways of being.

In *The Leadership Challenge*, James Kouzes and Barry Posner outline five practices common to successful leaders, maintaining that they "challenge the process, inspire a shared vision, enable others to act, model the way, and encourage the heart" (1987, p. 8). Influencing school leaders to increase their effectiveness in these domains is the most difficult form of coaching, as we are helping our coachees change *who they are*. This poses different challenges from simply teaching someone new knowledge and skills.

Can people learn new ways of being, or are our personalities, dispositions, and interpersonal skills fixed? If you are going to serve as a coach, you need to be very clear in your response to this question. Effective coaches believe firmly that people are capable of making fundamental internal changes. Research on these questions is consistent with common sense. Recent studies, particularly studies of identical twins raised separately, indicate that a big part of who we are is genetically determined. In fact, it is estimated that about 50% of what is commonly called personality is fixed in our genes. It is not unusual for twins raised in different environments to end up in similar professions and to have similar tastes and identical gestures and idiosyncrasies.

Dispositions, personality, and interpersonal skills are not fixed, however. Environment and experience play major roles in determining these in each of us. While nature may predispose us to take certain paths in life, nature gives us plenty of room to maneuver. Research in the field of neuroscience has clearly demonstrated that even old dogs can learn new tricks, that our brains (and our ways of being) are remarkably plastic. And the good news is that education professions provide us with tremendous opportunities for learning new ways of being, for expanding our repertoire of possibilities.

Here are a few examples of ways in which experienced educators report they have been personally transformed through their work:

- *"When I first entered administration, I had little confidence in myself, and I rarely spoke up at management meetings. When I did speak up, it was only after mentally rehearsing every word I was going to say. Now I am recognized as a leader among my peers and they can't shut me up!"*

- *"I'm an older white male and probably not the most nurturing sort. I had to learn to slow down and to listen and empathize as I work with students who are misbehaving, perhaps students who have real trauma in their backgrounds."*

- *"I am an introvert. I dread schmoozing at school parties or the Rotary luncheon. But I had to learn to do it to succeed in the job, and now I sometimes find myself really enjoying it."*

- *"For years I avoided raising concerns I had with some of my teachers. I was afraid of conflict, afraid of damaging my relationship with these teachers and my reputation for being a nice guy. I have finally learned how to lay out my expectations and raise concerns comfortably."*

- *"Every time the superintendent called with a parent complaint, I was a basket case. I was sure my job was on the line and that I had done something wrong. Now I understand that this comes with the territory and that every one of these interactions is a potential learning experience."*

- *"I grew up in a white, middle-class home and went through schools that were less than diverse. But I studied Spanish in high school, and served in Guatemala in the Peace Corps. I'm principal of a school that serves mostly Mexican immigrants. I'm not Latino by birth or upbringing, but I believe that I am a genuinely bicultural person."*

THE POWER OF TRANSFORMATION: TRIPLE-LOOP LEARNING

We have a colleague who rode her first "century," a one-hundred-miles-in-one-day bike journey, at age 55. At this point in her life, she is not a 56-year-old woman who rides a bike; she is a 56-year-old *bicyclist*. Bicycling has become a part of her way of being.

Becoming a bicyclist did not happen overnight. It occurred through incremental steps over time, starting with short rides, encouragement from friends, increasing distances, and most importantly, the declaration, "I can and I will do this." Through this transformational process, our friend has not only become very fit; she is now a person who has a hard time imagining a life without bicycling.

The process of transformation typically progresses through three stages:

- We gain new knowledge, skills, or ways of acting, in incremental steps.

- As we experience success with these new ways of doing things, we begin to change our way of thinking; we imagine a new context for these incremental changes; and we begin to reframe our sense of possibilities.

- As our new knowledge, skills, and ways of acting become transparent to us—integral to who we are—and as we see the world differently, our learning is fully integrated. We are transformed.

In *Masterful Coaching*, Robert Hargrove (1995) describes this process as *triple-loop learning*. He defines transformational coaching as a process that moves people beyond improved performance (single-loop learning), to developing new ways of thinking (double-loop learning), and ultimately to changing their ways of being (triple-loop learning). This framework has also been used by Peter Senge (1990) and others to describe levels of organizational learning.

Single-loop learning occurs on the instructional side of the Möbius strip of Blended Coaching Strategies. It is the place where incremental improvement occurs, where learners try out new knowledge, skills, and strategies. Facilitative coaching strategies, on the other hand, are directed at producing double- and triple-loop learning. At the double-loop level, learners begin to reshape their patterns of thinking, internalize new possibilities, and practice taking on new challenges independently. At the triple-loop level, the learner has integrated the new learning and embraces a new identity in relation to the challenge at hand. When this analysis is taken from the individual to the institutional level, we talk about moving an organization from adopting new rules or procedures to developing new systems and—ultimately—building new cultures.

Let's explore these concepts in relation to learning to play the piano. At the single-loop level, a learner might learn to tap out a few simple tunes from memory. At the double-loop level, a learner can read music with some fluency and is able to pick up new tunes, perhaps with some struggle, by reading music and practicing independently. At the triple-loop level, the learner is a musician—able to read, play, and compose with fluency and confidence. Figure 11.1 provides a schematic of the triple-loop learning process.

It is a dynamic process, and assumes that personal transformation is linked to and dependent on changes in how we act and what we think.

Table 11.1 provides several examples of triple-loop learning as it might apply to school professionals.

ONTOLOGICAL COACHING AND COGNITIVE BEHAVIORAL THERAPY: FOUNDATIONS FOR TRANSFORMATIONAL COACHING

Transformational coaching is informed by two closely related disciplines, *ontological coaching* and *cognitive-behavioral therapy*. Ontology is the study of being, and, in particular, the investigation of the nature of being human. In developing ontological coaching, Rafael Echeverría and Julio Olalla (1992) have examined the role of language in shaping human experience and

FIGURE 11.1 ● The Triple-Loop Learning Process

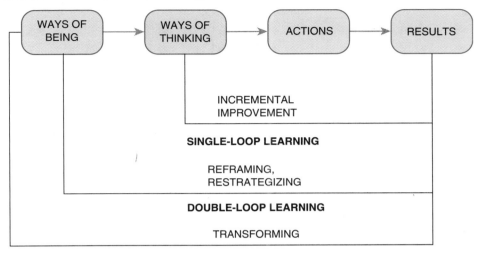

Source: Adapted from Hargrove (1995, p. 28).

TABLE 11.1 ● Triple-Loop Learning Examples

SINGLE-LOOP	DOUBLE-LOOP	TRIPLE-LOOP
Scenario 1: Latinx parents are currently not involved in decision-making at Suburban School. Kim, the principal, has no experience with Latinx students or communities		
Kim schedules site council meetings in the evening and provides child care in an effort to increase attendance.	Kim creates a Latinx parent steering committee in order to develop meeting agendas and strategies for engaging parents.	Kim is relaxed when immersed in the Latinx community. She seeks out opportunities to engage outside of the school setting. She is empathetic with recent immigrants and passionate in advocating for their interests.
Scenario 2: Jack avoids dealing with the school budget. He believes that he is "bad at math" and that the budget is "not about instruction."		
Jack sits down with his administrative assistant and reviews the budget.	Jack develops a monthly budget review and an annual budget planning process. He takes the school budget to the site council and staff for input.	Jack develops a deep understanding of the importance of aligning resources with his school vision. He asks difficult questions about how dollars are spent and develops systems for planning, evaluation, and allocation of funds. He is not intimidated by his multimillion-dollar budget.

(*Continued*)

(Continued)

SINGLE-LOOP	DOUBLE-LOOP	TRIPLE-LOOP
Scenario 3: Formerly a teacher at Isla Negra School, Rick has recently been appointed principal at the same site. Several teachers are not teaching the adopted curriculum. Rick is struggling with making the transition from colleague to leader		
Rick begins doing "quick visit" observations and asks teachers why they are not using the adopted materials.	Rick helps to create and facilitate grade-level planning groups that will support the implementation of the adopted curriculum.	Rick has a clear vision and expectations, and he communicates them consistently through processes such as professional development, school planning, and supervision. His personal identity has shifted to one of instructional leader among his former peers.

behavior. Building on the work of Humberto Maturana in the field of perception (Efran & Lukens, 1985) and the work of John Searle in linguistics (1969), Echeverría and Olalla illuminate the ways in which our interpretations of reality, embodied through language, shape our ways of being. A coach observes how individuals construct interpretations and narratives. An ontological coach helps individuals build new interpretations and narratives that open up new possibilities. In attending to our coachees' use of language and their interpretations of reality, we are able to provide a different perspective that may create opportunities for personal transformation.

Coaching is not therapy, as we have noted. However, as professional coaches we have much to learn from therapists. The overall track record of talk therapy is questionable; some researchers maintain that talk therapy is no more effective over time than placebos or no treatment at all. The one form of talk therapy that produces fairly consistent positive outcomes, however, is cognitive-behavioral therapy. This is an approach that has much in common with ontological coaching and with what we call transformational coaching.

Cognitive-behavioral therapy assumes that maladaptive behaviors, moods, and emotions can result from ways of thinking and perceiving. This approach is based on the notion that the way in which an individual responds to a situation is shaped by "automatic thoughts," or learned responses, and personal interpretations. Cognitive therapists attempt to help patients recognize and change dysfunctional thinking patterns and replace undesirable behavior patterns with positive ones. This approach to therapy is congruent with the triple-loop learning model.

Ontological coaching and cognitive-behavioral therapy rely on conversations between the coach or therapist and the coachee or patient in order to disclose narratives or thought patterns that are dysfunctional. Both disciplines also ask clients to try out new ways of being through exercises such as

- *Cognitive rehearsal.* The client imagines a problem situation, and the coach or therapist guides him through a problem-solving process that leads to resolution.

- *Role-playing.* The therapist or coach constructs role plays that allow the client to experiment with new ways of being.

- *Validity testing.* Clients are asked to test the validity of their assessments, interpretations, and narratives, providing evidence that they are true or false, functional or dysfunctional. Journals may be used in this process.

- *Homework assignments.* Clients are asked to try out ways of acting and being in the "real world."

How do these approaches link to Blended Coaching Strategies and to transformational coaching? As we work with our coachees to develop their capacity as school leaders, we often start in the instructional mode, at the level of single- and double-loop learning. But our goal has to be to move toward the deeper growth that is represented as triple-loop learning. Triple-loop learning requires the development of new ways of seeing and interpreting things and demands that we practice new ways of being. Developing new ways of seeing, interpreting, and being is at the heart of both ontological coaching and cognitive-behavioral therapy and forms the essence of transformational coaching.

Reflection: What might cognitive rehearsal, role-playing, validity testing, and homework look like in the context of leadership coaching?

THE BASIC MOVES OF TRANSFORMATIONAL COACHING

The ultimate goal of the coaching process is triple-loop learning and personal transformation. We hope to support the emergence of self-actualized professionals who have built internal capacity—self-reflective practitioners who take responsibility for their own professional growth. There are many models of what might be called transformational coaching in the literature. These frames may use different language, but generally they share the following common elements.

Start From Breakdowns. Here we remind you once more of Michael Fullan's adage: "Problems are our friends" (1993, p. 21). Every conflict, failure to achieve a goal, or crisis of competence is a learning opportunity. When a coachee acknowledges a problem, that coachee creates an opening for coaching.

Of course a coach must be selective, with input from the coachee, when determining which problems should be the focus of any coaching conversation. And it is critically important—as we point out in Chapter 12—that the coach work with the coachee to see beyond immediate, superficial problems to issues that are fundamental and systemic.

PRINCIPAL: Sandy [a teacher] is making me crazy.

COACH: Tell me about that.

PRINCIPAL: She is so preoccupied with her personal problems that she is neglecting her students and stepping all over our expectations here.

COACH: What is your history with this?

Listen to the Coachee's Stories and Test Them. As we have discussed, the ways we behave in the world are shaped by our interpretations of events, the stories we create to explain things. By definition, interpretations are subjective. Interpretations of the past and present shape future actions in ways that may be more or less functional. The fulcrum of transformational coaching is the act of helping a coachee become aware of her narratives and to explore alternative and more powerful ways of making sense of the world and behaving in relation to it.

PRINCIPAL: Sandy is a long-time teacher here, and she really does have some difficult personal issues she is dealing with. She was my friend before I even came here, so I know her pretty well. I have talked to her about some of the problems I have observed—being late to class, missing staff meetings, failing to supervise her kids, weak lesson planning—but things don't change.

COACH: Why do you think things haven't changed?

PRINCIPAL: Well, Sandy has a lot going on in her personal life. I don't think that she gets it.

COACH:	Tell me about your communication with her about this.
PRINCIPAL:	It has been frustrating. I try to be supportive. I let her know that I am worried, that as her friend I understand her problems, but that she needs to deal with these school issues.
COACH:	I hear you dealing with this as a personal issue, that you are both concerned and supportive as a friend. Can you imagine tackling this situation from a different role or point of view?

Use Data to Shift the Coachee's Perspective. Data can range from a coach's own observations, to the results of surveys, to research demonstrating that the coachee's conclusions may be incorrect. Each of these can play a critical role in helping a coach challenge a coachee's stories and interpretations.

PRINCIPAL:	I am afraid that if I confront Sandy about these issues, she'll collapse emotionally and the staff will blame me. Many of them really sympathize with Sandy.
COACH:	Let's refer back to that 360° instrument we did with your staff a few months ago. Do you remember what that survey told us about how you are perceived by your staff?
PRINCIPAL:	Well, they were pretty supportive.
COACH:	Yes, they were. The majority of respondents expressed a high degree of confidence in your leadership. You have a lot of capital with your staff. I recall there were also several comments suggesting that you need to be consistent with students and staff, that sometimes you give different messages to different people.
PRINCIPAL:	I remember that. Maybe I do need to be clearer with Sandy.

Develop and Test Interpretations and Strategies that Could Help the Coachee Deal Successfully With the Breakdown. What is there about the coachee's current way of being that is preventing her from moving forward? What assessments is she making about the situation or herself that are keeping her from taking effective action? What interpretations are the coachee holding that limit her possibilities, and how might they be shifted? Answers to these questions may not be immediately apparent, and a coach should explore alternatives with the coachee, testing out a variety of perspectives that could lead to movement.

COACH: I have an idea about what might be going on here, and I'd like to share it with you. It has to do with your own identity in this situation. Are you OK with me exploring this with you?

PRINCIPAL: Sure.

COACH: I am wondering if you are having a hard time playing the supervisor role. I know that you value your collegial relationship with your staff and in particular your history of friendship with some people, and I suspect you fear that if you hold Sandy accountable, it will jeopardize those relationships.

PRINCIPAL: There may be some truth to that...

COACH: I also suspect that it is not easy for you to play the supervisor role, which you hesitate to be the "bad guy."

PRINCIPAL: I hate being the bad guy.

Help the Coachee Construct New Interpretations, New Stories that Open up Possibilities for Effective Action. In *Masterful Coaching*, Robert Hargrove (1995) suggests that coaches help their coachees turn "rut stories into river stories." The first step is for the coach to "recognize and interrupt the rut story" and help the coachee to "understand the nature of the rut story" (p. 65). A rut story is an identity or interpretation of the world that limits possibilities. In this case, our coachee is stuck in the rut of wanting to be seen as humane and collegial. This prevents her from functioning as a supervisor and leader, and, therefore, from doing the right thing for her school. Hargrove says that once a rut story is named and understood, a coach can work with a coachee to build and practice a "river story," a new interpretation that allows for effective action (pp. 63–65).

Here the coach is beginning to help the coachee explore the possibility that if she holds Sandy accountable, she will be seen as an effective leader rather than as a "bad guy":

COACH: So you tell yourself that to be a supervisor, and to hold Sandy accountable, you will have to be the "bad guy" and that people won't like you as a result.

PRINCIPAL: There is an element of that in this situation. I am trying to build a positive culture here.

COACH:	What are the consequences of the "you-as-bad-guy" story?
PRINCIPAL:	Well, it leaves me pretty paralyzed. Sandy is still doing her thing, and I am kind of conflicted about it.
COACH:	OK, so let's try building a different story. Let's start with the way you would be perceived by staff. Rather than being seen as a bad guy for holding Sandy accountable, is it possible that your actions could be appreciated? What would that look like?
PRINCIPAL:	I suppose that some staff members are frustrated by having to deal with Sandy's rowdy students in the hallways, and they resent the fact that she misses meetings and such. They might appreciate it if I took this on.

Use Hypothetical Situations and Role Playing to Help the Coachee Practice New Ways of Being. A coaching conversation is an opportunity to test out new interpretations and new ways of being. Mediational questions can lead a coachee to explore new possibilities at the cognitive level and can even lead a coachee to project herself emotionally into an imagined scenario. Situated in the protected space created by the coaching relationship, the coachee can rehearse new ways of being.

COACH:	What would it be like for you to take off your old colleague hat and put on the supervisor/leader hat—and to be very clear with Sandy about your expectations?
PRINCIPAL:	I've tried that, but I guess I haven't been too effective. I always find myself backing off.
COACH:	So let's do a couple of role plays. In both, I'll play Sandy. In the first, I want you to be the hesitant you. But in the second, put on the supervisor/leader hat.

Create Possibilities for the Coachee to Practice New Ways of Being in the Real World. Transformation happens over time and through practice. Most change of this nature is gradual rather than cathartic. Our principal's growth as a supervisor and leader will occur incrementally, as she gains confidence and experience exercising this new role. It is important to take steps to ensure that commitments made in coaching conversations to exercise new ways of being are fulfilled outside those conversations. Coachees should agree to practice their new learning, and coaches should help them follow through by asking coachees to report back on their experiences during subsequent sessions.

COACH: How about if right now you develop a plan to meet with Sandy to outline your concerns and to lay out your expectations?

PRINCIPAL: OK, I'll ask her to meet with me after tomorrow's staff meeting. I suppose I should start by sharing the problems I've observed, then get real clear about what needs to change.

COACH: Let's write down specifics of the problems you plan to share with her and what you expect from her in the future.

PRINCIPAL: I think I'll start with supervision issues. Twice in the last week she has released her students…

The conversation continues until a concrete plan for the meeting with Sandy is established.

COACH: How can I support you with this meeting? I could help you plan it; I could observe it and give you feedback; I could debrief with you after it's over. I can do one, two, or all of these things.

DISPOSITIONS, EMOTIONAL INTELLIGENCE, AND TRANSFORMATIONAL COACHING

Dispositions are the soul of intelligence, without which the understanding and know-how do little good.
—David Perkins, author and founder of Harvard's Project Zero

Robert is a middle-school biology teacher. He knows his subject matter; he has a Master's Degree in botany and worked in biotech before getting his teaching credential. But 40% of his students are receiving D's and F's in his class. Despite extensive professional development aimed at helping him to meet the needs of his students, his teaching hasn't really changed, and Robert blames his students' failures on poor preparation and motivation.

Stephanie is a third year principal at a K-8 school in a middle-class neighborhood. She knows instruction and recognizes that her school, despite its relatively high test scores, is not serving its special education and English-learner students as well at it should. Yet she avoids getting into the classrooms of her mostly older and change-averse teachers.

Jan knows every one of her 29 students well and tries to make a personal connection with each of them every day. Her class is demanding and her standards are high, yet students love her. Jan, a 30-year-old teacher, participates fully in professional development, and welcomes collaboration with and feedback from her colleagues.

Successful educators possess a broad base of professional and content knowledge. Robert has a deep understanding of biology content, knows the science content standards, and aced the pedagogy classes in his preservice program. Yet Robert is not succeeding as a teacher, perhaps because he doesn't truly believe that all of his students are capable of learning his subject, or that it is his responsibility to insure that they do so. Stephanie was an outstanding teacher and understands differentiated instruction, models for meeting the needs of English-learners, and has a vision for establishing a Response to Intervention model at her school. Yet Stephanie is not leading her school forward because she is afraid of the conflict that might be produced if she were to communicate her expectations to her staff.

Jan, on the other hand, produces consistently outstanding results. Yes, her class is well organized, her lessons are well planned, and her pedagogy is effective. But arguably even more importantly, the atmosphere in her classroom and her relationships with her students build engagement, trust, and motivation.

Surely, effective teaching requires a high level of technical knowledge and skill. For example, the Model Core InTASC Professional Standards for Teachers include

Standard 1: Learner Development

Standard 2: Learning Differences

Standard 3: Learning Environments

Standard 4: Content Knowledge

Standard 5: Application of Content

Standard 6: Assessment

Standard 7: Planning for Instruction

Standard 8: Instructional Strategies

Standard 9: Professional Learning and Ethical Practice

Standard 10: Leadership and Collaboration (CCSSO, 2013)

The Professional Standards for Educational Leaders includes these standards areas:

Standard 1. Mission, Vision, and Core Values

Standard 2. Ethics and Professional Norms

Standard 3. Equity and Cultural Responsiveness

Standard 4. Curriculum, Instruction, and Assessment

Standard 5. Community of Care and Support for Students

Standard 6. Professional Capacity of School Personnel

Standard 7. Professional Community for Teachers and Staff

Standard 8. Meaningful Engagement of Families and Community

Standard 9. Operations and Management

Standard 10. School Improvement (NPBEA, 2015)

By and large, these standards outline job responsibilities that are operational in nature and that are traditionally taught through preservice programs, through professional reading, professional development, and on-the-job practice. In the Blended Coaching model, these are "ways of doing" likely to be supported through instructional coaching. As we are discussing, we bring Transformational Coaching to "ways of being," and the concept of Emotional Intelligence is a valuable perspective as we work to develop effective educators.

The term "Emotional Intelligence" was popularized by Daniel Goleman in his 1995 book by that name. The notion that Emotional Intelligence is essential to leadership, and to teaching, and that attention to social and emotional learning has a place in our schools and classrooms, is now widely accepted. Perhaps less accepted is the idea that coaches and supervisors educators must attend to and directly address emotional intelligence as they work in their support roles.

Goleman breaks Emotional Intelligence into four general categories:

1. *Self-Awareness*: Are you aware of your own strengths and weaknesses? Are you mindful of your own emotional reactions, your predjudices, your blind spots? Are you comfortable enough in your own skin to address your weaknesses, to be vulnerable and open to change?

2. *Self-Management*: Are you able to manage your emotions, to monitor your impact upon others, to behave appropriately as situations warrant?

3. *Social Awareness:* Are you aware of others' emotions, of the social dynamics that surround you? Are you sensitive to the impact that your presence and actions have upon others?

4. *Relationship Management:* Are you able to build and maintain relationships that will contribute to your and your organization's well-being? Are you able to communicate, persuade, and lead others?

Here are a few examples of educators who are working through challenges in the domain of Emotional Intelligence:

- Sam is struggling with personal issues, and on bad days is detached from his students and easily irritated and angered.

- Reyna is insecure about her teaching and avoids receiving feedback from her peers and supervisors, and when she does receive feedback she reacts defensively.

- Henry is a white male principal with a staff mostly made up of women of color. He is unaware that he is sometimes perceived as arrogant and patronizing.

- Principal Monica is self-assured, confident, and not what you would call warm and fuzzy. Many members of her staff miss the positive comments, inquiries into home life, and birthday recognition they received from Monica's predecessor.

The related topic of *self-care* is worthy of a mention here. Education professions can be physically, intellectually, and emotionally exhausting. Some educators are so committed to their work that they will deplete their well-being in order to serve what they perceive to be their job responsibilities. Coaches can help their coachees to understand that maintaining physical and mental fitness is a prerequisite to serving their communities well. Coaches are not therapists and must set appropriate boundaries around their coachee's personal issues. But, professional coaches can and should help coachees to strategize around issues of personal priorities, time management, and physical fitness. And they must be prepared to suggest that their coachees receive support from other medical and/or mental health professionals when challenges fall outside of the scope of coaching.

In many institutional cultures, these sorts of issues do not get addressed, beyond saying "this is a problem, get over it." Many institutions avoid giving them explicit attention. Coaches and supervisors must recognize that dealing with *ways of being* fall within their realm of responsibility, and understand that these issues are as important as issues of technical practice. How might a coach support each of these individuals?

- *Sam is struggling with personal issues, and on bad days is detached from his students and easily irritated and angered.* Sam is having trouble compartmentalizing his personal troubles, and is not fully aware of the impact he is having upon others. His coach shares, in a nonjudgmental way, the impact he is having upon his students based upon classroom observations and student interviews. He asks Sam to reflect upon these data and to develop an action plan for managing his moods. He reminds Sam that the district offers an Employee Assistance Program should he desire additional support. He suggests a few strategies for relationship building with students such as greeting them individually at the door and calling two families every evening with a positive report.

- *Reyna is insecure about her teaching and avoids receiving feedback from her peers and supervisors, and when she does receive feedback she reacts defensively.* Reyna's principal prefaces her conversation with her with reassurance that she sees Reyna as a "keeper" with true potential to be an outstanding teacher. She shares her expectation that Reyna will participate in peer observations, and her belief in the importance of professionals being able to discuss the good, the bad, and the ugly with one another. She offers to videotape Reyna teaching a lesson, and to debrief with her in a manner that will feel safe and professional.

- *Henry is a white male principal with a staff mostly made up of women of color. He is unaware that he is sometimes perceived as arrogant and patronizing.* Henry's coach shares this feedback with him in a nonjudgmental manner, grounding it in 360° survey data and her own observations. She asks Henry to reflect upon this information, which he receives with some surprise and a promise to address. They agree that she will observe Henry facilitate his next staff meeting for the purpose of helping Henry to become more aware of the behaviors that may be driving staff perceptions.

- *Principal Monica is self-assured, confident, and not what you would call warm and fuzzy. Many members of her staff miss the positive comments, inquiries into home life, and birthday recognition they received from Monica's predecessor.* Monica's coach shares this feedback, gleaned through the rumor mill, with her. Monica acknowledges that the feedback may be valid and agrees to do something about it. Monica and her coach role play simple "small talk" and then go to the staff room to give it a try. Monica's coach helps her to develop a plan for staff recognition that includes small individual and group celebrations.

The bottom line is that students perform for teachers they like and teachers they believe care about them, and adults are no different. Teachers and principals who demonstrate self-awareness, self-management, social awareness, and relation-ship management are far more likely to be successful than those who do not, and their coaches must be prepared to support them in developing and exercising those emotional intelligence competencies.

Dispositions are related to and different from emotional intelli-gence. Dispositions describe the ways in which we are inclined to think, make interpretations, and react. They are driven by our core values and beliefs, our upbringing, and reside at a deep level in our personas. For example, there is a teacher on almost every staff who has a disposition to love and care for natural things, and that is the one students bring naked, ugly, half dead fledglings who have fallen out of a playground tree to, knowing that that teacher will try to nurse that fledgling to adulthood.

Professional Standards provide a roadmap of evidence-based practices for teachers (InTASC, 2013) and school leaders (PSEL, 2015). But a list of professional practices does not work in isolation of an individual's dispositions and emotional intelli-gence. For example, the Council of Chief State School Officers (CCSSO), through its Interstate Teacher Assessment and Support Consortium (InTASC), "developed Model Core Teaching Stan-dards that outline what teachers should know and be able to do to ensure every PK-12 student reaches the goal of being ready to enter college or the workforce in today's world. The standards outline the principles and foundations of teaching practice that cut across all subject areas and grade levels and that all teachers share" (InTASC, 2013). The InTASC also suggests that teachers should be able to perform a wide range of professional functions, possess a large body of professional knowledge, and have a strong set of critical dispositions. Among those dispositions is the belief that all children can learn, respect for and valuing of diversity, belief that knowledge is not fixed but is complex, culturally situated, and ever evolving. CCSSO suggests that teachers must be disposed to commit to collegial planning, to adapting instruction to learning responses and needs, and to being a thoughtful and responsive listener and observer.

The Professional Standards for Educational Leadership (PSEL) for school leaders also address dispositions. Each standard begins with a statement such as "Effective educational leaders strive for equity of educational opportunity and culturally responsive practices to promote each student's academic success and well-being" and "Effective educational leaders cultivate an inclusive, caring, and supportive school community that promotes the academic success and well-being of each student."

A professional educator should probably know how to set up a classroom seating chart or plan a staff meeting agenda. But underlying and shaping those tasks is a set of dispositions or leadership practices that effective coaches and supervisors observe for, give feedback around, and help their coachees to be mindful of. As is the case with Emotional Intelligence, dispositions, in our Blended Coaching model, fall into the category of "ways of being," fundamental inclinations that may shape professional practice and that must be addressed through the supervision process. How might a coach respond to these scenarios?

- *Susan* has previously screened students into her Advanced Placement English class through an essay and interview. She is now being required to accept all students who apply, in an effort to increase participation by students from a low socioeconomic background and students of color. She is convinced that these students are being set up for failure.

- *Mario*, principal of Big High School, is quick to recommend expulsion or referral to continuation school for students who are perceived as disruptive and/or credit deficient. "These kids aren't going to make it here and getting them out is for the greater good."

- *Ralph* has been teaching intermediate students for 25 years and is well regarded in the community. He has seen "education fads come and go" and is a passive/resistant blockade to all new curriculum and professional development initiatives.

- Principal *Irene* believes that the working-class, immigrant parents at her school care about their kids, but don't have much to contribute to decision-making at her school site beyond occasional fund-raisers. However, categorical program guidelines require that parents have input in school decision-making.

In each of these cases, old habits, strongly held core beliefs, even what we might identify as elements of personality, are impacting professional performance. Susan may not be convinced that all students can learn, and may not be committed to her responsibility, as a professional educator, to produce equitable outcomes. Mario may be quick to dismiss some individuals because he lacks an understanding of and empathy for the challenges that some of his students have faced. Ralph believes that he has been successful and that that is enough. He does not see himself as a life-long learner, and resents those who ask him to examine and change his practices. Irene cares about her community, but in a patronizing way that is dismissive of the many contributions that community might make to the school's academic program and culture.

Some might argue that Susan, Mario, Ralph, and Irene are not about to change their dispositions; that our dispositions, by the time that we are adults, are pretty well fixed. But there is a large body of evidence to support the notion that, while our dispositions are deeply rooted, they can change in the right circumstances. There is also strong evidence (largely through the discipline of Cognitive Behavioral Therapy) that the best way to support people in evolving their dispositions is not through persuasion but rather through coaching people to change their behaviors, with the understanding that their beliefs may follow.

So how might we work with Susan, who is convinced that students who are not prescreened into her AP class are being set up for failure? A ham-fisted approach might be to tell Susan that she is expected to make this happen, that it is written into the school plan, that she will be monitored for her students' failure rate. One might directly challenge her dispositions, suggesting that she might not truly believe that all students can learn and that she is complacent about racially disproportionate outcomes. These steps are likely to fail, producing only a disgruntled teacher who will wait out and possibly undermine this initiative. Here are some steps a coach might take with Susan:

1. Acknowledging that Susan is committed to student success as evidenced by the high AP pass rate of her prescreened students.

2. Coaching Susan to develop a narrative suggesting that because of Susan's commitment to students, she would like to see more students, including students from a low socioeconomic background and students of color, participate in the AP program.

3. Listening and responding sincerely as Susan shares her doubts, complaints, and needs.

4. Coaching her in developing a strategy for implementing the mandate.

5. Working with Susan and administration to develop an opportunity for a slow start to the program, perhaps beginning with one class and Susan's commitment to work with a small case-study group of new AP students.

6. Arranging for Susan to have the opportunity to visit and observe teachers who have successfully implemented open enrollment AP courses.

7. Helping her to identify resources for after-school tutoring and other supports for AP students who would benefit.

In this example, we are not expecting Susan to change her beliefs coming out of the gate. At best we are hoping that Susan, while skeptical, will at least feel supported in attempting to implement a mandate. With a bit of luck and after a year or two, Susan will have a few success stories and her dispositions will shift.

When we work with folks like Susan, Mario, Ralph, and Irene, we are not likely to make much headway by directly challenging their dispositions. Rather, as coaches, we are more likely to be successful if we acknowledge that their intentions are good but that their outcomes need to improve, and if we work with them in implementing incremental changes in behavior that will produce positive results and hopefully shifting dispositions.

Imagine a principal with an IQ of 120 who is a master of all the knowledge, skills, and abilities outlined in the PSEL Standards. This principal has outstanding credentials and years of experience. But he does not really believe, in his heart of hearts, that all students can learn. He does not actually trust or respect teachers. How effective would you expect this imaginary principal to be?

Effective educators are fueled by commitments, beliefs, and passions. Michael Fullan calls this *moral purpose*.

Resource C.2 contains a Dispositions Self-Assessment for use by coaches and coachees. We suggest that coaches use this tool with their coachees and talk explicitly about the core beliefs and commitments that help principals get out of bed every morning and take on their difficult jobs.

Reflection: Can you identify a time in your own professional history when your beliefs or dispositions changed in a way that impacted student achievement? Can you identify a "rut story" that leaves you stuck, and can you articulate a "river story" that opens up different possibilities?

BRINGING IT ALL TOGETHER

In Chapters 6 through 11, we have explored the concept of Blended Coaching Strategies as a way of structuring coaching interactions. We suggest that coaches nurture change in a coachee's "ways of doing" and "ways of being" by using both instructional and facilitative coaching strategies. Working from instructional and facilitative stances, coaches may take consultative, collaborative, transformational, or other approaches. Table 11.2 illustrates the relationship between these approaches, and the next figure, The Blended Coaching Dance, illustrates the fluid interactions we call Blended Coaching (Figure 11.2).

TABLE 11.2 • Blended Coaching Strategies

COMPARING INSTRUCTIONAL & FACILITATIVE COACHING STRATEGIES		
	INSTRUCTIONAL	FACILITATIVE
Each primarily addresses...	Ways of doing... • *How can we challenge our gifted students?* • *What do I do with all of this student data?*	Ways of being... • *I get uptight every time I have to meet with the gifted parents.* • *Can we really close the achievement gap?*
And supports the development of...	Knowledge and skills... • *Proven models for differentiation in middle school classrooms* • *Templates for the presentation and analysis of student data*	Dispositions and internal capacity... • *A passionate belief in the school's obligation to every student* • *Self-reflection and ongoing learning through the process of leading school improvement*
Through the exercise of...	The basic coaching skills of • Building trust and rapport • Listening • Observing • Questioning • Providing feedback • Summarizing and committing to next steps	
And basic moves such as...	• Analyzing the knowledge and skills required to complete a task • Getting permission to instruct • Sharing examples, models, resources, methods, and information	• Paraphrasing, clarifying, asking mediational questions • Guiding reflection upon feedback • Examining assertions and assessments

(Continued)

(Continued)

COMPARING INSTRUCTIONAL & FACILITATIVE COACHING STRATEGIES		
	INSTRUCTIONAL	**FACILITATIVE**
		• Developing problem-solving skills • Shifting the locus of control to the coachee
Particular approaches include but are not limited to...	**Consultative coaching** • The coach shares his/her expertise and may collect and analyze data, outline options, and share suggestions	**Transformational coaching** • The coach facilitates a processes aimed at producing deep personal transformation in the coachee
	Collaborative coaching • The coach uses both instructional and facilitative approaches as the coach and coachee work together in a master/apprentice relationship to complete a project	
A skillful coach orchestrates a fluid, blended, reiterative process...	**Blended Coaching Strategies**	

FIGURE 11.2 ● The Blended Coaching Dance

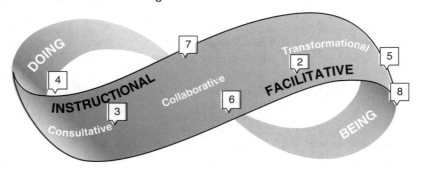

In Figure 11.2, we highlight a sequence of selected coaching interventions over several sessions, as Mara supports John, a high school principal in leading improvements in Algebra instruction at Ringwood, a large comprehensive high school.

1. *Setting the Stage*: Mara and John set an agenda for their work together, revisiting goals and commitments from previous sessions, touching on current concerns, and planning for their time before every session.

2. Using *facilitative* methods, Mara helps John to clarify his concerns and goals in relation to Algebra instruction. Mara does this by asking John to share his narrative, paraphrasing, and asking clarifying and mediational questions. She also uses facilitative coaching to help him identify teacher leaders and the communication processes he'll use to involve the faculty and parent community in addressing his goals.

3. In the *instructional consultational* mode, Mara identifies a number of potential sources of student data that should be useful to John, and shows him how to interpret the data. She also provides John with templates of department meeting agendas that other schools use to plan and monitor program improvements.

4. In the *instructional* role, Mara researches potential model programs for Ringwood, and recommends a site for visitation and the employment of a consultant to assist the mathematics department leadership team.

5. In the *facilitative* role through facilitative questioning and probing paraphrasing, Mara leads John through the process of identifying potential barriers to the implementation of an improvement plan.

6. John and Mara visit mathematics classrooms at Ringwood, and Mara uses *facilitative* questioning to help John to ground his assessments of the instructional practices observed and to outline next steps. She uses *instructional* coaching as she shares ideas for school-wide professional development strategies with John.

7. Mara uses both *instructional collaborative* and *facilitative* moves as she and John *collaborate* in finalizing the plan for Algebra program improvement that will be taken to the Curriculum Council for approval.

8. Mara leads John through a *facilitative, transformational* coaching role-plays to prepare him for difficult conversations with the few parents and teachers who oppose the changes.

9. *Summarizing*: Every meeting is closed by a review of the conversation and recording of next steps and commitments.

Coaching is a complex process that is often informed by intuition. None of us will become accomplished practitioners by reading a book or attending a workshop. We can learn to be effective coaches by approaching it as we do any challenging discipline, through ongoing practice and feedback from colleagues in our shared professional learning community.

Reflection: Next time you have coaching conversation, bring a copy of the Möbius graphic along, and chart your conversation as you move between instructional and facilitative strategies. What do you observe about your own coaching?

PART III

Coaching in Support of School Improvement

In Part I, we outlined the value of coaching as a tool for the professional development of educators, and we discussed the basic skills that coaches should possess. In Part II, we illustrated the application of two fundamental coaching strategies, facilitative and instructional coaching, and the uses of collaborative, consultative, and transformational approaches to coaching in a fluid, blended process. Table 11.2 illustrates the ways in which these concepts and practices interact.

In Part III, we bring all of this together through a discussion of the importance of using coaching to drive systems improvement. We advocate for a supervision model that is grounded in coaching. We discuss the components of quality leadership coaching and professional development induction programs, and we share a variety of resources intended to help individuals and organizations that are interested in building such programs.

CHAPTER 12

Coaching-Based Supervision

WHY COACHING-BASED SUPERVISION

We're going to make a few assertions here that are well substantiated by research and K-12 thought leaders:

- The single most powerful variable in school success directly subject to our influence as K-12 educators is teacher quality.

- The second most powerful variable is almost certainly principal quality.

- Historically, we have done a poor job of monitoring and improving educator efficacy through the supervision process.

- We have done a poor job of supporting teacher and principal professional development through the supervision process.

The word supervision is derived from root words meaning "to see from above." Supervision is the act of overseeing a person or activity. Thus, supervision implies hierarchy; the supervisor has knowledge and/or power that the supervisee does not. In most school districts, teacher and principal supervision is strictly defined in negotiated agreements and in board policies and job descriptions. In the education world, peers don't supervise peers, and supervisors have the power to direct their supervisees.

To evaluate is to assign value. In the world of teacher and principal supervision, to evaluate is typically to make judgments about strengths and weaknesses in professional performance, and often to assign ratings. While "supervision"

FIGURE 12.1 ● Blended Coaching Supervisory Feedback Model

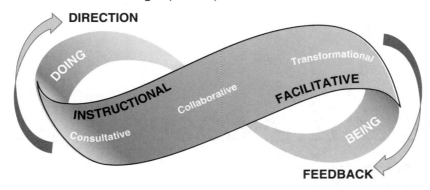

implies hierarchy, evaluation does not. A peer, a stakeholder, or a third party can evaluate. That being said, the formal act of principal and teacher supervision is typically confined to those in supervisory roles both by negotiated agreements and district policies and procedures. Supervision and evaluation serve two primary purposes, purposes that are sometimes complementary and sometimes in conflict with one another, to ensure acceptable professional performance, and to support improvement in professional performance.

Supervision and evaluation processes determine who receives permanent status, who is promoted, who is disciplined. In some systems, supervision and evaluation processes drive merit pay schemes. Just as importantly, supervision and evaluation processes should support institutional growth and individual professional growth. Through engagement in the process, supervisors are informed about and influence institutional performance and culture, and are in the position to help individuals to improve their professional practice.

We won't go into detail about the history of teacher supervision and evaluation here, other than to say that the most important influences on the current practices are the innovations of clinical supervision, professional standards for educators, walk-throughs, the accountability movement, and the influence of collectively bargained agreements.

The clinical supervision model was first proposed in the 1950s by Morris Cogan and suggests that teachers be evaluated primarily through a formal evaluation process that includes a preobservation conference, a classroom observation, and a postobservation conference. Formal observations structured along the lines of the clinical supervision model remain at the heart of most teacher supervision and evaluation processes in the United States.

Perhaps because the formal observation process promoted by the clinical supervision model provides a very incomplete picture of teacher practice, more informal, short classroom walk-throughs by supervisors have become common, a practice promoted by Carolyn Downey and others.

Professional standards for educators and their accompanying rubrics have become universal tools for judging educator performance. Charlotte Danielson's *Framework for Teaching* (1996) has served as the foundation for most teacher standards, and the Interstate School Leadership Licensure Consortium's principal standards (1996 and 2008) have informed principal professional standards across the United States, until they were revised as Professional Standards for Educational Leadership (PSEL) in 2015. The Framework for Teaching (2022) was recently revised and attempts to define practices that result in student and school success. The Framework for Teaching (FFT) philosophy is that by supporting teacher reflection, collaboration, inquiry, and innovation, the framework will have a direct impact on student learning and development. But professional standards have a glaring weakness in that they primarily describe adult behaviors, focusing our attention away from impact upon students and evidence of student achievement.

The accountability movement, fueled by research demonstrating the impact of teacher quality on student achievement, and by awareness of the achievement gap as illuminated by No Child Left Behind (NCLB), brought both pressure and attention to educator evaluation and supervision. Systems were revised to require the inclusion of student achievement data in the process. Value Added analysis was integrated into many systems, and various forms of merit pay have proliferated around the country. Race to the Top aspired to hold teachers accountable by using performance evaluation systems to measure such things as planning, classroom climate, instruction, professional responsibilities, and student achievement. The student achievement formulas varied from state to state. School administrators' performance was most often measured by determining school improvement goals and collecting data that could show progress on the goals. Most states included some measure of student achievement in order to show that the principal was successful in positively impacting learning. Unfortunately, what often occurred was a misalignment between the principal's goals for school improvement and the goals individual teachers selected to measure their effectiveness. In 2015, the Every Student Success Act (ESSA) was established and prioritized local control of educational decision-making. There is still an expectation that there will be accountability and action to effect positive change in the lowest performing schools, but districts and states will determine how educators will be held accountable for student success.

In the past, unions and administrator professional organizations have been reluctant partners in the design and implementation of supervision and evaluation models. Federal programs like No Child Left Behind and Race to the Top Acts provided financial incentives to spur and reward innovation and reform that improved educator performance resulting in approved student performance as measured by state assessments. More recently, the federal Every Student Succeeds act rewarded state and local education agencies who worked with their various local stakeholders including unions and professional organizations to create supervision and evaluation systems for K-12 that were less punitive and incentivized professional learning and educator growth and development. This is not to say that all systems are perfect and that as a result all schools are led by effective principals with an effective teaching staff. Also with the current crisis regarding teacher recruitment and retention, it is essential that K-20 systems that include state and local education agencies, institutions of higher education, professional organizations and unions collaborate to improve preparation, support, and professional growth programs for all educators.

Historically, across the country, around 98% of teachers are rated as effective or higher by existing evaluation systems, despite clear evidence that student achievement is less than satisfactory in more than 2% of our classrooms (2013 NY Times See source in comments). Perhaps of even greater concern than our failure to confront poor performance is the fact that most teachers receive little or no direct feedback on their performance, and most report that they have not grown professionally as a result of the evaluation process.

And although changes in performance evaluation systems across the country have resulted in increasingly focused educators' attention on classroom instruction, new evaluation systems, however, have not consistently resulted in greater differentiation among teacher performance ratings. Differences in underlying teacher effectiveness alone cannot account for why 1% or fewer teachers are below proficient in Hawaii but 28.7% are below proficient in New Mexico, or why only 6% of teachers in Georgia and 9% of teachers in Massachusetts are above proficient but 62% meet this higher standard in Tennessee (Educational Researcher, v. 46, n. 5, pp. 234–249, Jun–Jul 2017. 16 pp.).

The argument can be made that the hierarchical model of supervision is flawed and that education professionals should move to a peer supervision model similar to that seen among some other professionals. We believe that this argument has merit and are long-time supporters of peer supervision and support approaches. But for a variety of reasons, it seems clear that a traditional hierarchical approach to supervision in K-12 is here to stay. Unfortunately, K-12 educators remain stuck in a place where they are not quite true members of a profession. Working conditions, compensation, poor preservice programs, broader social and cultural issues, and other factors militate against the recruitment of a highly qualified, diverse, and capable body of professionals.

There is a tension between the advocates of nonhierarchical supervision and evaluation and advocates of seemingly objective judgment-driven, top–down models. In their book *Supervision That Improves Teaching and Learning*, Sullivan and Glanz (2013) argue that "bureaucratic inspectional supervision should have no place in schools in the 21st century" that we should move to a "democratic" model recognizing that "teaching is complex and not easily defined or understood" (p. 35) and that "supervisors function best when they pose questions for critical analysis by teachers." This runs counter to the results-driven teacher accountability models that proliferated under NCLB.

Both approaches ignore the day-to-day reality in our nation's schools. The reality is that for the foreseeable future, principals will supervise and evaluate teachers, and superintendents and assistant superintendents will supervise and evaluate principals. For the foreseeable future, teachers, principals, and superintendents will be overworked and stretched thin. Some will be outstanding performers, some will be flat out incompetent, and most will be somewhere in the middle. Many of our students will continue to fail despite our stated commitment to "close the achievement gap." In the end, the most powerful mechanism we have for insuring that those incompetent educators leave the profession, that the outstanding ones stay, and that those in the middle improve in order to better serve our students, is the supervisor/supervisee relationship.

A recent study (Grissom, Egalite, & Lynsay, 2021) that was focused on the effect principals have on students and schools concluded that principals have large effects on student learning, approaching even the effects of individual teachers. Replacing a principal at the 25th percentile in effectiveness with one at the 75th percentile can increase annual student learning in math and reading by almost three months, annually. These findings are significant. Replacement may not be an option in hard-to-staff schools and districts. We suggest that providing support, high-quality professional development, and coaching-based supervision is a better alternative to removing a principal before trying to improve their skills and knowledge. In some cases the individual may need to be removed, but the priority should always be to support and grow the principal first. If supervision and evaluation could be structured in a way to be more supportive and focused on improvement, many principals may have developed the skills they needed to be effective school leaders. Assistant Principal and Principal candidates who are fresh out of preservice preparation programs have completed what we might call basic training. They will build on this knowledge and skills as they practice in schools with their first assignment. This is why coaching support is so important. A coach can structure coaching sessions for the novice principals or assistant principal on areas of identified need for professional growth.

Figure 12.2 illustrates key findings from Grisson, Egalite, and Lindsay's (2021) study. Effective principals focused on three skill areas that included People, Instruction, and Organization. They understood human development and demonstrated relationship skills such as caring, communication, and trust building. Principals who were effective had skills in instructional pedagogy and were able to support teachers' classroom instruction. These principals were also good managers who used data to inform decision-making, were strategic in their problem-solving, and used resources efficiently. Effective principals applied leadership behaviors that align to the PSEL such as engaging in instructionally focused interactions with teachers (Standards 4 & 6), facilitating professional learning communities (Standard 7), and building a safe and productive climate (Standards 1–10). A coach can target these skill areas and behaviors when working with an assistant principal or principal to grow and improve their leadership skills.

So given that teacher and principal efficacy are critical to student success, given that we are not doing a good job of professional supervision in K-12 to date, and given that a hierarchical approach to supervision is not likely to change soon, we have some work to do. If supervision and evaluation are to lead to improved performance, one of the barriers that

FIGURE 12.2 ● Skills and Behaviors of Principals Impacting School Improvement and Student Achievement

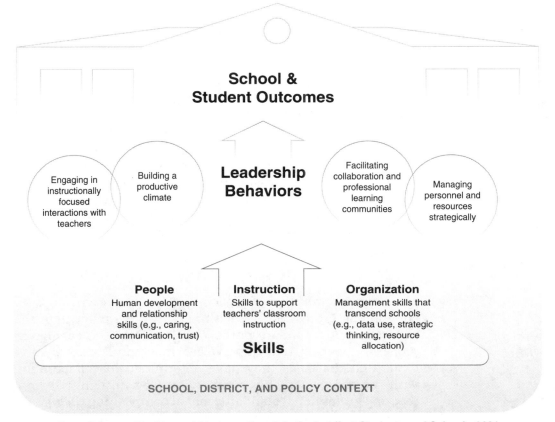

School & Student Outcomes

Engaging in instructionally focused interactions with teachers

Building a productive climate

Leadership Behaviors

Facilitating collaboration and professional learning communities

Managing personnel and resources strategically

People
Human development and relationship skills (e.g., caring, communication, trust)

Instruction
Skills to support teachers' classroom instruction

Organization
Management skills that transcend schools (e.g., data use, strategic thinking, resource allocation)

Skills

SCHOOL, DISTRICT, AND POLICY CONTEXT

From Grissom, Egalite, and Lindsay, *How Principals Affect Students and Schools*, 2021

● U R B A N ● I N S T I T U T E ●

Source: Grissom, Egalite, and Lynsay (2021).

we have to overcome is what we will call the Coaching v. Supervision Myth.

THE COACHING VERSUS SUPERVISION MYTH

Can supervisors coach their supervisees? In many domains, this would be an absurd question. Medical residents are taught, supervised, and evaluated by attending physicians. So are junior attorneys in law firms. Within the military, senior officers train and supervise those who are lower on the hierarchy, and evaluate their charges in order to assign responsibilities and determine who is eligible for promotion. Ironically, in K-12, where the myth that one can't both coach and evaluate persists, coaching and supervision live side-by-side in many situations. Basketball coaches help players improve their performance by providing them with feedback and suggestions, while also deciding who makes the team and who comes in in the third quarter. Effective Calculus teachers help their students to learn difficult concepts, providing individual support on lunch breaks and during class time, while at the same time being responsible for assigning grades and writing college recommendation letters.

So effective coaches supervise in the sense that they "watch from above." In fact, it is the ability to bring a new perspective to the coachee and to provide feedback that makes coaching valuable. But coaches don't have the power to direct. Supervisors do. For the purposes of this conversation, let's use the Webster definition of supervision, *the action or process of watching and directing what someone does or how something is done*, with the understanding that supervisors have the power to evaluate and influence the job status of the supervisee.

DEFINING COACHING-BASED SUPERVISION

The primary purpose of Coaching-Based Supervision is to support the professional growth and effective practice of the supervisee. A secondary purpose is to inform the evaluation process, ensuring that supervisees meet professional standards and the goals they have determined in collaboration with the supervisor. When supervisees are in danger of not meeting professional standards and accomplishing their goals, the focus of supervision may shift away from coaching to accountability and to personnel or disciplinary actions.

The Blended Coaching model is the foundation of Coaching-Based Supervision. All of the skills and strategies inherent in the model are brought to the supervision process. Additional strategies brought to the table, strategies that are not available to a pure coach, are the ability of the supervisor to provide Supervisorial Feedback and Supervisorial Direction.

SUPERVISORIAL FEEDBACK

All feedback from a supervisor is high stakes. Human beings are hardwired for hierarchy. There is plenty of research with primates both hirsute and human that demonstrate our tendency to look for and defer to authority. We look to our boss, chief, priest, rabbi, professor, mother, or team captain for direction, affirmation, and feedback. Feedback from a supervisor, an individual higher up in the hierarchy, is powerful, and almost always carries more weight, positive or negative, than feedback from others.

Feedback from a coach or mentor who does not have hierarchical authority may also have gravity, gravity grounded in the respect and regard the mentee has in the mentor or coach. But there is no explicit power or threat underlying that feedback.

There are some good reasons for a supervisor to think twice before sharing feedback with a supervisee, among them:

- A supervisor's casual feedback may be interpreted as criticism or direction.

- In giving feedback a supervisor preempts the supervisee's opportunity to discover the data/situation/concern on their own.

- In sharing feedback, the supervisor promotes their own priorities, possibly undermining the leadership and ownership of the supervisee.

Perhaps this is why some authors suggest that supervisors who are attempting to take a coaching stance should somehow separate their coaching interactions from their evaluative interactions. But this is impossible, and unproductive. From a supervisee's perspective, feedback from a supervisor, even if that supervisor purports to be wearing a "coach hat," always carries the extra weight of feedback from the boss. And from the supervisor's point of view, it is unrealistic to suggest that information and interactions taking place in a somehow compartmentalized "coaching" session will not inform the evaluation process. So while supervisors using a coaching-based approach can and should provide feedback, they should do so in a thoughtful way, mindful of the potential impacts, both positive and negative, of that feedback.

CHARACTERISTICS OF EFFECTIVE SUPERVISORIAL FEEDBACK

- It is specific.
- It is grounded in evidence.
- It is tied to explicit goals, expectations, and/or standards.
- It is linked to impact upon students, teaching, and learning.
- It communicates that the supervisor has the supervisee's best interests at heart and believes that growth can occur.
- It is bold but never mean spirited.
- It is delivered in an invitational manner and at a time and in a place where it is likely to be heard.

- It is not personal; it focuses upon practices and behaviors.

- While not personal, it addresses issues of personal style, dispositions, equity, and relationships in relation to outcomes.

- In the feedback conversation, the supervisee is coached to reflect upon the feedback and to think through their actions in response to the feedback.

- The supervisor asks for feedback from the supervisee regarding the conversation from the supervisee.

TYPES OF SUPERVISORIAL FEEDBACK

Feedback can come in many forms. At some level, every interaction between a supervisee and his/her supervisor conveys feedback in the form of facial expressions, how quickly the supervisor returns a call, and how the supervisor responds to what he or she has seen or heard. The most effective feedback is delivered deliberately and with an end in mind. Here are a few examples of types of feedback:

- Direct observations made by invitation. *You asked me to observe for students being on task. Three boys in the back of the room...*

- Direct observations of supervisee behavior. *You appeared to be defensive in responding to Mrs. Jones...*

- Direct observations of the ways in which others respond to supervisee behavior. *Mrs. Jones escalated when you did not acknowledge her concern...*

- A supervisor's own reaction to supervisee behavior. *You seem very distracted to me and I don't feel like I am being listened to...*

- Judgment grounded in data. *Your school has a very high rate of assigning students to special education. Here are the numbers for your school compared to similar schools...*

- Judgment grounded in perception and standards. *We see things differently. I don't agree that this meets grade level standards. Let me explain why...*

- Judgment in the form of summative evaluation. *I am rating you as "Needs Improvement" in this area based upon this evidence...*

In a weak traditional supervision model, feedback is dumped into a supervisee's lap, and that is the end of it. In a Coaching-Based Supervision model, feedback is just the beginning of the conversation, a conversation in which the supervisor coaches the supervisee in response to the feedback.

In this first snippet of dialogue, Judy shares feedback with Brian from a traditional boss' stance:

JUDY: I have been in your classroom three times in the last few weeks and I haven't seen you using the cooperative learning strategies we have agreed to implement here.

BRIAN: Sorry, I have been trying some of them but you have missed those times.

JUDY: I'll try to get in again. Let me know a good time to drop in.

Judy is missing an opportunity here. Judy is communicating an expectation of compliance, but is not interested in taking the time to understand where Brian is in relation to trying out cooperative learning strategies, let alone to support him in developing his competence. Here, Judy goes deeper, taking a coaching stance building upon her supervisorial feedback:

JUDY: I have been in your classroom three times in the last few weeks and I haven't seen you using the cooperative learning strategies we have agreed to implement here.

BRIAN: Sorry, I have been trying some of them but you have missed those times.

JUDY: So you have been experimenting with the strategies a bit. Which ones have you tried, and how have they worked out for you?

BRIAN: I do "think-pair-share" a bunch... I've really been doing that sort of thing for a long time.

JUDY: Can you identify another one of the strategies you would like to try out? I can come in and observe you and provide feedback, if that would be helpful.

Supervisees and supervisors who are paying attention recognize that there is subtle feedback embedded in almost every interaction. The topics that a supervisor chooses to ask about provide feedback about that supervisor's priorities. The ways in which a supervisor reacts to what a supervisee has to say, from body language to explicit statements, are feedback to that supervisee. In fact, every supervisor/supervisee conversation is rich in feedback between parties, and both parties should be mindful of this fact. When a supervisor is preparing to provide important feedback to a supervisee, he or she might want to plan the interaction with the following questions in mind:

- What do you perceive as an area for growth, action, concern?
- What evidence do you have to support that perception?
- How does this link to explicit goals, standards, expectations, and teaching and learning?
- What relevant history or other factors are related to this issue?
- When and how can you provide this feedback so that it is received productively?
- What do you want as the outcome of this interaction?
- Outline the statements you will make in providing this feedback.
- How will you coach your supervisee to develop an action plan in response to the feedback?
- How will you follow-up on this conversation and the commitments that both you and the supervisee make?

ON SUPERVISORIAL DIRECTION

We have defined supervision as *the action or process of watching and directing what someone does or how something is done* with the understanding that supervisors both evaluate and influence the job status of their supervisees. We argue that effective supervisors can increase the capacity of their supervisees by building coaching relationships with them. And we know that as supervisors, their feedback to supervisees carries more weight than it otherwise would, and that as supervisors they cannot surrender their rights and responsibilities to provide direction.

Professional educators operate with a high degree of autonomy on a day-to-day basis. Supervisors can't ride on their shoulders telling them what to do; as we have discussed, what they can do is use a coaching-based process to strengthen their capacity to perform independently. That being said, sometimes supervisors must step up and provide direction.

WHEN IS SUPERVISORIAL DIRECTION APPROPRIATE

- When failure to act jeopardizes safety, legality, student interests, or the immediate job security of the supervisee

- When the supervisor has been unsuccessful in helping the supervisee to arrive at a key decision or to take effective action through a coaching approach
- When an institution is implementing a mandate
- When an action or decision must be taken and it is expedient to "just do it"

CHARACTERISTICS OF EFFECTIVE SUPERVISORIAL DIRECTION

- It is tied to explicit goals, expectations, and/or standards.
- It is time specific, and monitoring and accountability for implementing the direction are explicit.
- The direction and follow-up are documented appropriately.
- Once the direction has been articulated, the supervisor works with the supervisee from a coaching stance to develop an action plan.
- The supervisor provides the supervisee with appropriate support needed in order to implement the action plan.

Let's go back to Judy and Brian, and take a look at an example of Supervisorial Feedback and Supervisorial Direction. In this scenario, let's assume that Brian has a long history of failing to implement agreed upon school-wide teaching strategies.

JUDY: I have been in your classroom three times in the last few weeks and I haven't seen you using the cooperative learning strategies we have agreed to implement here.

BRIAN: Sorry, I have been trying some of them but you have missed those times.

JUDY: So you have been experimenting with the strategies a bit. Which ones have you tried, and how have they worked out for you?

BRIAN: I do "think-pair-share" a bunch... I've really been doing that sort of thing for a long time.

JUDY: Your department agreed to do a jigsaw activity around one chapter using expert groups, with individual and group accountability. I expect you to give that strategy a try next week.

BRIAN: I just haven't had the time to plan that lesson.

JUDY: What do you need in order to try a jigsaw next week?

BRIAN: Maybe I can ask Suzette to share her lesson plan.

JUDY: What date and time can I come and see this in action? What would you like me to look for?

After observing Brian trying a jigsaw lesson, she has the opportunity to put on her coach hat. She can ask Brian to reflect upon the lesson and its impact upon students. She can ask coaching questions that lead him to develop a plan of next steps in relation to implementing cooperative strategies. And she can lay out her clear expectations (her Supervisorial Direction) to Brian as he moves forward with those next steps.

There are plenty of reasons to be careful in sharing supervisorial feedback and direction. Educators are often quite insecure, both because it is virtually impossible to be a perfect teacher or principal, and because we invest so much of ourselves, our egos, our sense of worth, in our work. Educators are "people persons," and we hesitate to share feedback that might hurt someone's feelings or produce "push back." We are not recommending here that you be, in the words of Phil Jackson, an asshole. But we are recommending that you be bold as both a coach and as a supervisor. Withholding difficult feedback and direction can be a huge mistake, a mistake that damages students, supervisees, and your relationship with your supervisees.

Your students suffer when poor performance is left unaddressed. That first grader gets only one shot at a successful first grade experience, and if it doesn't go well, the experience may shape her entire life trajectory. That high school teacher who has poor student engagement in his classroom may not even realize that a significant percentage of his history students lack the reading skills necessary to pass his class.

Your supervisees suffer when poor performance is left unaddressed. Nobody comes to work in the morning intending to do a poor job, but many come to work with weak skills, bad habits, or flagged motivation. Many of us are unaware of our weaknesses and will thankfully address them when they are pointed out. Some become locked into a cycle of "phoning it in," knowing that their performance is weak, perhaps blaming students or others, having no fun or fulfillment. A supervisor's job is to help his/her supervisee to experience success.

Your relationship with your supervisees suffers when poor performance is left unaddressed. It may seem that you are buying peace by failing to share difficult feedback with a supervisee, but you are also losing respect, and missing out on the opportunity to build trust by sensitively and appropriately sharing difficult feedback with your supervisees. And remind yourself of who really loses when poor performance goes unchecked. It is the students who are on the receiving end when principals and teachers do not perform effectively.

Your relationship with your staff suffers when poor performance is left unaddressed. Generally speaking, your staff knows where the problems lie. When supervisors appear to ignore performance issues, motivation and respect suffer among those staff members who feel that they are giving things their all.

Consider these examples of Coaching-Based Supervision in action:

Example 1: Jack was a long-time mathematics teacher at Central High School. He had played basketball at the school as a student, and now coached the sport. He was the teacher union's chief negotiator. And he had a higher failure rate in his algebra classes than his colleagues. He had reportedly stated that Mexican students (an increasing portion of the population at Central) simply weren't good at mathematics. And he had received positive evaluations for the past 35 years.

Jenny was the new principal at Central, and was appalled by the school's poor record of preparing students, particularly Latinx students, for admission to four-year colleges and universities. Algebra was clearly a key "gatekeeper" course in this context, and she knew she had to deal with Jack and the mathematics department. But would it be smart for a new principal to take on an established union leader and member of the "old guard"?

Jenny chose to be bold. She produced class by class and teacher by teacher data showing evidence of mathematics achievement, pass rates, and grading practices. She disaggregated the data by gender and race. She conducted frequent walk-throughs in mathematics classrooms. And she sat down with Jack sharing these data grounded in the assumption that he wanted to do the right things for his students. This led to Jack's spending time observing colleagues, participating in a variety of professional development activities, and ultimately retiring early, expressing a great deal of respect for Jenny.

Example 2: George was a new principal at Oak Middle School. His supervisor Carlos met with him at his site for the first time in September, and noted that he referred to his administrative assistant as "darling" and referred to a young teacher as a "girl." Even though this was Carlos' first substantive encounter with George, he did not hesitate to point out George's language to him and ask him how it might be interpreted and what repercussions might result. George reflected upon Carlos' observations and quickly changed his behaviors.

TRANSFORMATIONAL COACHING AND COACHING-BASED SUPERVISION

The Blended Coaching model recognizes that "ways of being," issues of emotional intelligence and dispositions, are central to the success of K-12 educators. As discussed in Chapter 11, we propose Transformational Coaching as a key strategy in addressing these issues. Transformational Coaching is central to the work of coaching-based supervision.

Suppose you are supervising an educator and you recognize that his or her potential for growth lies not primarily in learning a new curriculum, a new piece of software, or a new way of designing lessons or of structuring interactions with students, but rather in transforming his or her "way of being." Perhaps your supervisee is challenged by his or her relationships with colleagues or students, or is lacking in motivation or commitment. How can you support that individual in his/her personal growth? Here are some of the actions that are available to you in taking on a transformational supervision challenge:

1. *Identify the challenge.* Typical challenges that call for transformational coaching fall into the domains of emotional intelligence and/or dispositions. If your supervisee has the self-awareness and willingness to be vulnerable to identify the challenge themselves, so much the better.

2. *Gather evidence to substantiate the challenge.* That evidence may come in many forms. It may come in the form of interactions you have experienced or observed. It may come in the form of survey data. It may come in the form of failure to act or succeed on a professional initiative, or in the form of the supervisee's self-assessment.

3. *Frame the challenge in relation to standards and expectations, and in relation to impact upon students.* Prepare to take conversation beyond your personal opinions to frameworks such as Emotional Intelligence, teaching standards, and/or leadership standards. Understand the impact of the challenge upon students.

4. *Share explicit Supervisorial Feedback with your supervisee about the challenge.* Ground that feedback in evidence, tie it to standards and expectations, and to impact upon students.

5. *Share explicit Supervisorial Direction with your supervisee.* Be clear about the seriousness of the challenge and what you expect to take place as a result of this conversation.

6. *Ground a coaching conversation in your commitment to supporting your supervisee's success.* You have to sincerely believe that growth is possible, and communicate that belief.

7. *Provide your supervisee with opportunities to respond to and reflect upon the challenge you have presented.* This is where Facilitative Coaching comes most into play, as you paraphrase, ask clarifying questions, and push your supervisee's thinking through mediational questions.

8. *Listen for narratives that may be helping your supervisee to stay stuck.*

9. *Challenge those narratives and propose alternative narratives.* As you identify those narratives, test them with your supervisee, explore their implications, and find new, more productive ways to interpret things.

10. *Help your supervisee to find opportunities to try out new ways of being.* Among other things, you may role play with your supervisee, observe them in real-world settings, and expect your supervisee to step outside of their comfort zone.

EVALUATION MODELS THAT WORK

Evaluation models are those collections of requirements, timelines, and forms that drive the supervision of teachers and principals. These models are often codified in negotiated agreements, and are often grounded in the industrial labor model that is an anathema to coaching-based supervision.

There is no shortage of examples of failed evaluation models in the K-12 universe. Scratch the surface of most school districts and you will find teacher and principal evaluation processes that are often not implemented with fidelity if at all. Interview teachers and principals and many will tell you that they have not been evaluated on a regular basis, and that when evaluated, the process has not had a whole lot of value. Interview evaluators and they will often tell you that the process is burdensome and as much about filling out forms and meeting deadlines as it is about professional growth and accountability.

Coaching-based supervision will almost always be implemented within the context of an evaluation system that culminates in some sort of summative evaluation. The evaluation system itself may facilitate a coaching-based approach, or may put up barriers to a coaching-based approach. As you examine and perhaps consider revising your evaluation systems, you might look for these barriers to coaching-based supervision, barriers that are all too common in the field:

- The system is complex and requires the completion of multiple forms at the expense of encouraging meaningful conversation.

- The system requires participants to compile large quantities of "artifacts" and "evidence" rather than relying on shared observations and carefully selected data.

- At the heart of the system are ratings driven by pseudo-scientific quantitative points derived largely from test scores and other measures.

- The system relies on overly complex rubrics, and/or rubrics that do not make clear distinctions between levels. "Some," "a little bit," and "a lot" are not clear distinctions!

In contrast, an evaluation model that supports coaching-based supervision includes the following characteristics:

- *It is grounded in the belief that the primary purpose of supervision is to support improved performance.* Supervision is not about ensuring compliance so much as it is a process designed to support professional growth and efficacy.

- *While supervision is primarily about supporting improved performance, it is also a mechanism to insure that supervisees meet professional standards and are held accountable for their work.* Any system of supervision has to insure that students' interests are protected, thus even as professional growth is our primary goal, we have to guarantee that students are being well served.

- *The system is built upon a set of clear professional standards and expectations.* If we are going to support people in their growth, and hold them accountable for their performance, we have to have a clear understanding of what effective performance looks like. A quality classroom in 1950 looked different than a quality classroom in 2023. Our expectations of educators and our vision for effective performance are articulated in professional standards, and also in a variety of other contexts including school and district plans and negotiated agreements. Rubrics are clear and explicit.

- *Ratings categories articulate the fact that even successful educators are engaged in ongoing professional growth and focus upon goal attainment.* Most of us are "developing" in at least a few areas. Almost none of us "exceed standards" in all areas.

- *There is a branch of the system for those who do not meet standards and whose performance needs immediate improvement.* The improvement plan component provides for an explicit plan with clear timelines, outcomes, and supports.

- *The evaluation system is a priority, not an afterthought.* It is understood that growing and supporting staff members is of the highest priority, and that coaching-based supervision takes time. Thus, principals are not asked to supervise an overwhelming number of teachers, and they receive direct support so that they may spend their time as instructional leaders, not as office managers and disciplinarians.

- *The evaluation system is ongoing and integrates multiple inputs and data sources.* For classroom teachers, formal observations, informal observations, walk-throughs, formative and summative student data, student work, student and staff surveys, participation as a member of a professional learning community, all may inform the process. Gone are the days of two formal, preannounced observations every three years, a summative report and end of conversation.

- *The evaluation is iterative.* Each interaction builds upon prior interactions. Gone are the days where evaluation consisted of a semi-annual report card completed with no reference to prior work. The process is built around relationships rather than box checking.

- *The evaluation process is linked to goals.* A strong model is driven by evaluatee professional growth goals, student achievement goals, and program goals, grounded in school and district goals.

Many scholars in education believe that coaching can also help school leaders to enhance their leadership in order to improve schools and elevate districts to higher levels of achievement (Thach, 2002). In the past several years, there has been a growing interest in principal coaching as a significant component of principal professional development (Hobson, 2003; Reiss, 2006). Unlike other professional development programs, coaching can respond to the needs of the principal directly and enhance their ability to solve the complex problems they face every day (Neufeld & Roper, 2003). Most of us agree that a principal's leadership is essential in driving school improvement priorities. According to Goff, Guthrie, Goldring, and Bickman (2014), "As the focus of educational reform increasingly centers on school-level performance, research and policy attention have turned to the quality of principals as a potential pivot point for school improvement (Robinson, 2007)" (Robinson, 2007, p. 682).

CHAPTER 13

Coaching for Systems Change

> *Systems thinking is a body of knowledge and tools that helps us see*
> *underlying patterns and how they can be changed. It is these patterns*
> *that are roadblocks to change, not specific people or events.*
> —Nancy Isaacson and Jerry Bamburg

Our work as leadership coaches is about making a difference for students. In order to affect a lasting impact on student achievement, coaches have to help their coachees look beneath and beyond immediate problems to identify systemic causes and opportunities. Let's see what we find when we bring a systems perspective to Jeffers High School, a large urban school, and its principal, Paul:

PAUL: I'm pretty frustrated with my assistant principals. I have asked them to spend 30% of their time in classrooms in order to support teachers in implementing our writing across the curriculum initiative, but I don't see them in the classrooms— and I'm afraid many teachers are blowing off the writing initiative.

COACH: Let's focus on your APs for now. What do you think is preventing them from getting into classrooms?

PAUL: I'm just not sure if it is a priority for them. I'm not sure they know how to support teachers in teaching writing across the curriculum. What they'll tell you, though, is that they are tied up with discipline and campus supervision.

COACH: How have you dealt with your APs about this?

PAUL: I guess I need to ride them harder about getting into classrooms. I know they would like me to take things off their plates, but I don't know what that might look like.

At this point, a coach might be tempted to problem-solve with Paul about the supervision of his assistant principals, their professional development, and the ways in which their duties are assigned. This approach might tease out some strategies for an incremental change in the ways APs use their time, but it would bypass an opportunity to intervene on a deeper level.

A number of facts emerge as Paul's coach questions him about his APs and their role at Jeffers High School. It turns out that the APs process an average of 9,000 tardies, 900 teacher-generated discipline referrals, 1,200 work detail assignments, and 800 suspensions each year, most of which are for an accumulation of minor offenses such as tardies and dress code violations. Despite the presence of ten classified campus supervisors, the APs are expected to be on the yard at every break as well as before and after school. It's no wonder that the APs have no time to get into classrooms. It's also not a surprise that achievement data for the school are below those for schools with similar populations.

In helping Paul think about why his APs are not getting into classrooms, several deeply systemic issues emerge. These include the need to clarify the role of assistant principals as instructional leaders and to train and support them in exercising the role, the need to transform the school culture from one that pushes out noncompliant students to one that strives to regain their commitment to schooling, and the need to build administrative mechanisms that will reduce the amount of time administrators spend processing discipline issues.

Until the school takes steps to reduce the number of tardies, teacher referrals, suspensions, and work details, the APs will not have time to get into classrooms. Until the school takes on the cultural transformations that result in kids getting into class on time and in all teachers pulling their weight in dealing with discipline, student achievement at Jeffers High will not increase. As long as the school continues to suspend students for failing to dress for PE, and for accumulating tardies and such, many students will continue to be sucked into the cycles of failure that inevitably result in poor results on the exit exam

COACH   (referring to a rough chart he has drawn with Paul):
        So it looks like there are at least 15 significant factors
        tied to the difficulties that your APs are having
        getting into classrooms.

PAUL: OK, so it's not about me just telling my APs to get
        into classrooms more often, or just telling my
        teachers that I expect them to teach the writing
        curriculum.

COACH: I think you're right. It's far more complex than that,
        and dealing with this complexity offers far bigger
        payoffs. Where do you think you should go from here?

PAUL: What if we were to have some focus groups with
        students and teachers to think about ways in which we
        can reduce tardiness and suspensions? And I'm not
        talking about bringing in just the student council kids.

WHAT ARE SYSTEMS?

There are many systems at play in schools. Some contribute to a
school's ability to achieve its goals; some do just the opposite.
Some are formal, procedural systems, such as attendance tracking
and monitoring. Others are overarching, complex, and informal,
as in the relationship between teacher expectations, classroom
environment, and student attendance and achievement. Some
have been created through deliberate processes, while others have
evolved and exist by default. Often, systems are invisible to those
who are immersed in them. The coach, as a different observer, can
help the coachee to see both deliberate and default systems, to
evaluate their impacts, and to explore alternatives.

Systemic considerations such as resource allocation, professional
development, and the use of data in decision-making have an
impact on virtually every aspect of school quality. They overlap and
relate to one another synergistically. A school cannot implement an
effective system of continuous improvement processes, for
example, without also having effective data collection, analysis,
and communication systems in place. An effective system of professional development that addresses school needs will be difficult
to attain without an effective assessment system and a system for
articulating shared beliefs and vision.

What's the difference between an effective process and an
effective system? A professional development day in which
teachers look at assessment data, identify strengths and
weaknesses, and write up and turn in notes can be an isolated
procedural event. It can also be part of a larger systemic

initiative. Are there guidelines for the data analysis and collaborative processes? Does everyone involved know what the steps and timeline are? Do we know how we will measure our success and how often we will do it? Are there explicit processes in place to connect the examination of data to what happens in the classroom? Was this a one-time event, or can staff say, "We consistently do it this way at our school"? When a school has planned, communicated, and implemented the specific ways processes will work, we can say that a proactive systemic approach is being taken.

AN EXAMPLE OF COACHING FOR SYSTEMS CHANGE

Lydia approached her coach with a problem. She was not satisfied with attendance at the recent Homewood Elementary Back to School Night and was having trouble getting parents to volunteer for her site council. The parents of students of color were particularly underrepresented. She was frustrated; she just couldn't think of a way to get more parents to read the flyers that went home with students every week.

Lydia's coach resisted the temptation to help Lydia brainstorm better ways of getting publicity into parents' hands. Instead, the coach helped her recognize that her approach to parent communication had been haphazard. Together they explored the possibility that the school's culture and history of relationships with the community were inhibiting parent engagement. If Lydia was truly interested in increasing parent participation, she needed to develop a plan that went beyond improving parent notification and then implement and evaluate its impact. Lydia and her coach collaborated to come up with the action plan illustrated in Table 13.1.

This plan was implemented, and it began to have an impact on parent attendance at school events. The spring parent survey indicated that some parents felt that home–school communications had improved. However, the percentage of parents attending school events, volunteering, and even responding to the survey did not meet Lydia's expectations. Upon further reflection and conversation with parents, Lydia realized that many parents were not comfortable at the school and did not feel welcomed. The *superficial symptom* of poor parent attendance was the result of a *systemic failure* to create a culture that welcomed and valued parents. At the core of this problem was a teaching staff that had difficulty relating to the new immigrant groups that had moved to the school. Lydia worked with

TABLE 13.1 • Homewood Elementary Parent Publicity Plan

RECURRING NEED	PROCEDURES AND PROCESSES
Parents need timely access to basic calendar information	• All communications in English, Spanish, and Vietnamese • Master wall calendar in front office maintained by office manager • Annual calendar mailed to parents in May and September and included in all registration and visitor packets; copies available in office display rack all year long • Monthly newsletter mailed home that includes updated two-month calendar
Parents need timely access to information about schoolwide and special events	• All communications in English, Spanish, and Vietnamese • Phone calls and home visits by bilingual liaison to encourage participation by underrepresented families • Monthly newsletter mailed home that includes updated school activities and announcements • Every newsletter includes a *How to Reach Us* section, with phone numbers, school address, Website, and e-mail addresses • Parent information marquee in front of school maintained and updated weekly by PTA • Glass showcase on outside wall displays current notices for parents and community as well as school events and activities maintained and updated weekly by a staff representative with parent volunteer • Copies of notices, schedules, and flyers displayed on a wall rack accessible to visitors, regularly resupplied and updated by office assistant • Recording of school events, reminders, and dates available on answering voice mail, updated daily by office assistant • School Website provides access to all notices and schedules, updated weekly by Tech Coordinator, School Tech Club, and parent volunteers • Whiteboard with daily announcements maintained for all staff and parent volunteers; all staff can contribute announcements; office assistant cleans and monitors daily
Trends in parent participation will be measured so this plan can be evaluated and adjusted	• Parent evaluation of quality of home—school communication in annual spring survey • Input from site council • Measure trends in parent participation in key events and committees • Measure trends in participation of underrepresented parents

her coach, parents, and staff to implement a number of steps at the classroom, site, and community levels. While these—shown in Table 13.2—were not all directly related to parent attendance at school events, they resulted in much higher levels of participation.

TABLE 13.2 • Homewood Elementary Parent Publicity Plan

RECURRING NEED	PROCEDURES AND PROCESSES
Parents need timely access to basic calendar information	• All communications in English, Spanish, and Vietnamese • Master wall calendar in front office maintained by office manager • Annual calendar mailed to parents in May and September and included in all registration and visitor packets; copies available in office display rack all year long • Monthly newsletter mailed home that includes updated two-month calendar
Parents need timely access to information about schoolwide and special events	• All communications in English, Spanish, and Vietnamese • Phone calls and home visits by bilingual liaison to encourage participation by underrepresented families • Monthly newsletter mailed home that includes updated school activities and announcements • Every newsletter includes a *How to Reach Us* section, with phone numbers, school address, Website, and e-mail addresses • Parent information marquee in front of school maintained and updated weekly by PTA • Glass showcase on outside wall displays current notices for parents and community as well as school events and activities maintained and updated weekly by a staff representative with parent volunteer • Copies of notices, schedules, and flyers displayed on a wall rack accessible to visitors, regularly re-supplied and updated by office assistant • Recording of school events, reminders, and dates available on answering voice mail, updated daily by office assistant • School Website provides access to all notices and schedules, updated weekly by Tech Coordinator, School Tech Club, and parent volunteers • Whiteboard with daily announcements maintained for all staff and parent volunteers; all staff can contribute announcements; office assistant cleans and monitors daily
Trends in parent participation will be measured so this plan can be evaluated and adjusted	• Parent evaluation of quality of home–school communication in annual spring survey • Input from site council • Measure trends in parent participation in key events and committees • Measure trends in participation of underrepresented parents

It is easy to focus on superficial presenting problems without ever getting at systemic issues. It is the coach's job to help the coachee get out of the habit of "putting out fires" and instead to invest time and energy installing automatic sprinkler systems and removing fuel and sources of ignition.

Table 13.3 provides three more examples—from our own coaching experience—of presenting problems that principals have brought to us, the superficial causes that were the initial focus of our conversations, and the systemic causes that were at the root of the problems.

TABLE 13.3 • Systems Interventions at Homewood Elementary

LEVEL	INTERVENTION
Classroom	• All home–school communications from classroom teachers translated into home languages • Full-time translator made available to teachers for calls and conferences • All teachers have voice mail and stated expectation to return calls within 24 hours • All classrooms reflect multicultural themes • Quality of teacher/home communication a focus of the teacher supervision process • Teachers expected to telephone target parents to encourage attendance at conferences and other key events
Site	• Consistent disaggregation of classroom, grade level, and school-wide data by sub-groups and sub-group performance an ongoing focus of PLCs • Ongoing training and dialogue for all staff around diversity and community issues • Parent meetings at times determined by parents, with translation and child care • Purchase of multicultural classroom teaching resources • Recruitment of teachers and other staff members representative of the community • Ongoing measurement of parent participation and attitudes
Community	• Principal outreach to community groups and churches • Engagement of diverse community leadership in school improvement processes

COACHING FOR SYSTEMS CHANGE AND TIME MANAGEMENT

Most school leaders struggle with time management. The demands of the job seem overwhelming, and the dozens of interactions a school principal must engage in during any one hour make it difficult to take the long view. Steven Covey, author of *Seven Habits of Highly Effective People*, provides a useful frame for thinking about the relationship between leading systems change and managing time. Covey (1989) suggests our time is spent in four kinds of activities, as illustrated in Figure 13.1.

School leaders often become stuck in a cycle of responding to urgent issues, both important and not important. Systems solutions, on the other hand, are almost never urgent and are almost always important. A critical role for the coach, then, is to help the coachee carve out the time and the psychological space in which to do the important but not urgent work of identifying and implementing the structural interventions that will make a true and lasting difference for students.

Reflection: Review the three examples of problems and systemic issues above. Do you agree that the systemic causes we outline are important but not urgent? Can you think of ways in which the failure to address these systemic issues might produce problems that are urgent?

FIGURE 13.1 ● Four Types of Leadership Tasks

Urgent Not Important	Urgent Important
Not Urgent Not Important	Not Urgent Important

COACHING OUTCOMES

In coaching for systems improvement, the coach helps the coachee to:

- Look behind the presenting problem to the underlying causes of an issue

- Become skilled at identifying systemic problems that surface as minor issues

- Invest in systems improvements rather than short-term solutions

As school administrators gain experience, they recognize systems and become skilled at setting up new systems and tuning up old ones. Yet we vary in our ability to recognize and analyze systems. With coaching, coachees can become experts at implementing systems that will not only ensure that their schools run smoothly, but that will also provide the time and structures for instructional leadership.

> *Exercise:* Look at Table 13.4 on the next page. Read over the issues presented by the principal. Reflect on the superficial causes that the principal has assigned to the issues. What deeper systemic causes could be at play?

For each of these cases, imagine the ways in which you could use facilitative strategies to gain a better understanding of systemic causes. What steps could you take using a consultative approach to help you and your coachee have a better understanding of the facts? How could you work either collaboratively or in a facilitative mode to help a principal create and implement an action plan that would address the underlying problems? (See Table 13.5.)

In the face of immediate concerns, we often have difficulty "seeing" the systems at play. Systems analysis takes practice, both on the part of the principal and the coach.

COACHING INDIVIDUALS, GROUPS, AND INSTITUTIONS

The primary focus of this book is to support those who coach and supervise individuals. Those individuals are embedded in groups, and in larger systems, and it is not unusual for coaches

TABLE 13.4 • From the Superficial to the Systemic

ISSUES	SUPERFICIAL CAUSES	SYSTEMIC CAUSES
1. There are currently too many invalid referrals from classroom teachers to the school's Student Study Team (SST).	Staff members are not following the school guidelines for SST referrals.	There is no system for ongoing communication between special education and classroom teachers. Most staff lack a repertoire of differentiation strategies for academic and behavioral interventions. The culture of the school is one in which teachers view "special needs" students as "someone else's responsibility."
2. The principal is stressed about never having enough time to complete tasks or projects.	She is currently spending 60 minutes a day supervising recesses. She sees five to ten students each day who are sent to the office.	There is an outdated school discipline plan that has no clear system for office referrals. There is no system in place for substitute yard supervision, except default to the principal. The principal does not practice scheduling and prioritizing tasks.
3. A teacher at the school is not teaching the required English Language Development (ELD) lessons.	The teacher likes to teach physical education and is allotting 40 minutes a day to this subject area. The teacher claims she can't "fit everything in" to the curriculum.	The district lacks an adopted ELD curriculum with a system of assessment. The school has no consistent practice of collaborative curriculum planning and delivery.

TABLE 13.5 • Consider Underlying Systemic Causes

ISSUES	SUPERFICIAL CAUSES
1. The school budget is a "mess" with no clear information available for the principal to use in making decisions.	The secretary is new and has no budget experience. The district office budget printouts arrive late and are difficult to interpret.
2. An i3nfluential parent is complaining about a teacher not being accessible for questions, information, and conversations about her child.	The teacher in question does not have a phone in her room. The teacher coaches basketball in the afternoon and says she does not have time to meet with the parent.
3. For the third year in a row, target populations (Latinx and African American subgroups) have not met their achievement growth targets.	High staff turnover has had a negative impact on students at this school. An analysis of attendance data shows a higher rate of absenteeism among African American and Latinx students.

to be called upon to work with groups and even with broader institutional systems. Coaches might work with principal/ assistant principal teams, with grade-level teams and professional learning communities, with entire departments, or with governing boards. The basic coaching skills that we have outlined in this book apply in individual, group, and institutional coaching settings. Here are some ways in which coaching may evolve as it moves from individual to institution:

COACHING INDIVIDUALS
Instructional, Consultative, Collaborative & Facilitative/Transformational Strategies Goal and Feedback Driven Focus on Individual Performance
COACHING GROUPS
Instructional, Consultative, Collaborative & Facilitative/Transformational Strategies Goal and Feedback Driven Focus on Individual Performance
COACHING GROUPS
All of the Above Focus on Relationships, Procedures, Habits Mindful of Group Narratives
COACHING INSTITUTIONS
All of the Above Focus on Vision, Policies, Plans, and Contracts Intervene in Systems, Expectations, and Accountability Intervene in Institutional Culture and Narratives

Our point in this chapter is a deceptively simple one: the role of a school leadership coach is to move coaching conversations and interventions beyond the immediate issues to those underlying opportunities for systems improvement that are likely to have the greatest positive impact on students. It is often the norm that the principal wants a quick fix when a teacher or parent comes with a concern. The principal quickly assesses the concern and puts a "band-aid" on the problem. Unfortunately the principal has not asked enough questions, listened in an empathetic manner, or talked with his or her coach about the problem. What we suggest takes time and effort, and principals are busy people. The problem is that often the "band-aid" approach does not work and the concern or problem continues to be unresolved. So many times small concerns or complaints are consequences of ineffective systems within the school. A well-trained and experienced coach can provide the support to the principal and their team to work through these systemic issues that can be distractions to the instructional focus of the principal's day.

CHAPTER 14

Designing a Leadership Coaching Program

T he coach–coachee relationship is at the heart of a coaching-based leadership professional development program. A number of other considerations also impact program quality. These include the selection and professional development of the leadership coach and the structure and curriculum of the coaching process.

WHO SHOULD COACH?

Many hugely successful basketball and football players have tried their hands at coaching, and most of them have had less success as coaches than they did as players. Many first-class coaches were never top-tier players. What does this tell us about the relationship between being a school leader and becoming a school leadership coach?

QUALIFICATIONS AND SELECTION OF LEADERSHIP COACHES

One thing is very clear: exceptional school leaders are not necessarily exceptional leadership coaches. An individual who has a stellar reputation and track record as a principal or superintendent may not possess the interpersonal skills and professional knowledge required of a leadership coach. It is critically important that we be conscious of this, because school leadership coaches are frequently drawn from the ranks of retirees. Retirees are a remarkable resource, but potential coaches must be screened to ensure that they are a match for the work, just as they would be in any other high-stakes employment decision.

Must a coach always have experience in the coachee's job? In the private sector, CEOs work with executive coaches who have never served in the top seat. Many athletic coaches have never competed as players at the level of the teams they coach. Because we suggest a dynamic model of coaching that includes instructional strategies, we believe that coaches must have a firm handle on the knowledge and skills required of the individuals they are coaching, but a precise job match is not required. It isn't necessary to have been a high-school principal in order to coach a high-school principal (although it helps), but one should certainly have a strong grasp of the issues faced by high-school leaders and a vision for quality secondary education.

At times, a coach may be called upon to support a leader in a single focus area. In this sort of circumstance, expertise in that focus area (along with coaching skills) may be more important than possessing leadership experience in a role similar to that of the coachee. For instance, a high-school principal working to implement writing instruction across the curriculum may benefit from focused coaching by a literacy expert who has never served in a principalship but has extensive experience with professional development at the secondary level.

We suggest that at a minimum, school leadership coaches should meet the following qualifications:

- Five years of successful educational leadership experience;
- Evidence of successful informal mentoring relationships; and
- Evidence of appropriate dispositions, knowledge, and skills.

The selection process should require:

- The submission of letters of recommendation that specifically address the ability to serve in a coaching role;
- A formal interview which includes role-playing of coaching scenarios; and
- Reference checks.

Selection as a coach should be conditional upon:

- Completion of a training program;
- Participation in ongoing professional development that includes;
- Shadowing and being shadowed by an experienced coach; and
- Participation in a community of practice that meets regularly to reflect on current issues in serving as coaches.

"OUTSIDE" VERSUS "INSIDE" COACHES

As we illustrated in Chapter 2, we believe that school leaders need both internal and external supports in order to succeed in today's demanding environment. Ideally, a coach is part of the *external* support system.

An external coach is independent of a coachee's school system. She is able to assure the coachee of confidentiality. Her commitment is to serve the school system (which is usually the paying customer) by dedicating herself to supporting the success of the coachee *outside of the summative evaluation process*. This is particularly important given the political vulnerability of school leaders.

This is not to say that coaches should not be in communication with coachees' supervisors. Regular, three-way conversations among coaches, coachees, and supervisors are important in order to ensure that the professional development focus of the coaching work is aligned with the supervisor's perceptions and expectations. At a minimum, a coach should meet with their coachee and supervisor at the beginning of the school year to review goals and expectations, do a mid-year check-in, and end of the year review.

It is often difficult to establish programs in which coaches are "outsiders." Sometimes it is easiest for school districts to establish their own internal programs of coaching support for principals. Where this is to be the case, it is very important that the role of the coach in relation to the district be clearly defined—and the boundaries of confidentiality be established and maintained.

ONGOING PROFESSIONAL DEVELOPMENT FOR COACHES

Leadership coaching is a demanding and complex professional practice. Leadership coaches should come to their work well-prepared, with the recognition that to be a leadership coach is to be committed to one's own ongoing professional growth. Before serving in a coaching role, coaches should have initial training and experiences in the kinds of skills and strategies outlined in this book. But this background is only a foundation for what should be an ongoing learning process.

School leadership coaches should be engaged in the following activities as integral elements of their practice:

Maintaining Currency in the World of School Improvement. Leadership coaches (who, as we've noted, are often retirees) must stay on top of research, legislation, and current trends in the education community. They can accomplish this through reading, conference attendance, and by staying connected to the daily lives of school leaders.

Seeking Models and Feedback in the Real Work of Coaching. It is extremely valuable for novice coaches to shadow experienced coaches and to be observed by them as they coach. It should be our goal to build apprenticeship relationships that naturally evolve into collegial ones.

Acquiring New Approaches to Coaching. There is a good deal of literature and a vast professional development community concerned with executive coaching, particularly in the private sector. We encourage school leadership coaches to explore these resources.

Participating in Communities of Practice. It is essential that leadership coaches build communities of practice for one another. Such communities become places for shared problem-solving, for the learning and application of new strategies and skills, and for the general strengthening of professional practice.

Committing to Reflective Practice. Leadership coaches need to exercise the self-discipline of examining and reflecting on their daily practice. They should solicit feedback from those they serve and make time to unpack their self-observations. A journal can be a highly effective tool for this purpose.

Acknowledging the Barriers to Coaching Relationships. Leadership coaches should be aware that the individuals being coached may perceive coaching as counseling or need for improvement rather than a professional growth opportunity. Creating opportunities to address these concerns are essential for trust to occur between the coach and coachee.

FORMATIVE ASSESSMENT AS A FRAMEWORK FOR LEADERSHIP DEVELOPMENT

Effective professional development is organized around outcomes and, therefore, demands a clear understanding of the skills, knowledge, and dispositions we are trying to produce. The PSEL Standards articulate the vision on which our coaching is centered. It is the coach's job to help the coachee grow into the school leader described by the PSEL Standards (Figure 14.1).

Formative assessment is a continuous improvement cycle, one led by the coach but owned by the coachee. The cycle begins by taking stock of the coachee's context, needs, strengths, and weaknesses. The Resources section contains a sample tool for this purpose, a self-reflection assessment guide that can be completed by the coachee, the supervisor, the coach, and others. This guide is derived from the PSEL Standards. Other tools in the Resources section include a 360° survey instrument to gather perceptual data from subordinates and others. These might include prior years' evaluations, school data, and anything else that will help to identify a coachee's strengths and areas for growth as well as establish leadership priorities in the coachee's context. Some school

FIGURE 14.1 ● The Formative Assessment Cycle

districts provide principals and assistant principals the opportunity to participate in a Strengths Finder Assessment (Rath, 2007) which can be helpful in determining areas of focus for coaching sessions.

Leadership coaching should be organized around the accomplishment of explicit goals, goals that are aligned with PSEL Standards and informed by contextual data. Specific plans should be made to achieve them. One tool for this purpose is the Individualized Development Plan (IDP) shown in Figure 14.2 and included in Resource C.4. In districts where the performance evaluation process is aligned to the PSEL Standards, it is much easier to reference the performance goals as an initial starting place for coaching conversations. When a principal determines a goal for improvement and the supervisor will be monitoring progress of the goal, a Leadership Coach can focus coaching sessions on strategies to strengthen decision-making around that goal. For example, the principal has a goal to increase his participation in weekly PLC meetings where teachers are focused on improving questioning techniques. The Leadership Coach can work with the principal to identify resources that might be helpful and plan

FIGURE 14.2 ● Individualized Development Plan

INDIVIDUALIZED DEVELOPMENT PLAN (IDP)

STANDARD: ____________ COACHEE ____________

COACH ____________

ELEMENT OF THE STANDARD: ____________ SUPERVISOR ____________

		TIMELINE													
ACTIVITIES	PERSONS RESPONSIBLE	JUL	AUG	SEPT	OCT	NOV	DEC	JAN	FEB	MAR	APR	MAY	JUN	EVALUATION	DATE OF REFLECTION INQUIRY MEETING

I approve and will support the implementation of the IDP.

COACHEE ____________ Date ____________

COACH ____________ Date ____________

SUPERVISOR ____________ Date ____________

Source: Reprinted with permission from the New Teacher Center, https://newteachercenter.org

strategies for interacting and adding substantive feedback to the PLC team.

The IDP—negotiated between coach and coachee—outlines the key steps each will take and sets out a specific plan to achieve explicit goals. It is usually developed annually and is regularly revisited and revised. Present throughout the coaching process, it provides a focal point for ongoing examination of practice.

The IDP and the formative assessment process are distinct but not isolated from the process of formal, employer-based summative evaluation. Ideally, the summative evaluation process is organized around the same set of standards that form the basis for formative assessment, and the goals established in the IDP constitute the coachee's professional development goals for the purposes of summative evaluation. The coachee's supervisor participates in the formative assessment and IDP process, and evidence of progress through that process is considered in the summative evaluation. A coach might contribute to the summative evaluation process through a three-way conversation with the supervisor and coachee, discussing the year's activities and accomplishments. An external coach would not, however, share assessments about a coachee's performance with a supervisor.

We suggest that coaches use a Collaborative Log form—illustrated in Figure 14.3 and also included in the Resources section—at every coaching session, as a tool for organizing the coaching process, encouraging accountability on the parts of both the coach and coachee, and maintaining a record of coachee progress. The Collaborative Log is a simple form that brings discipline to the coaching process. Used in conjunction with standards assessment and the IDP, it brings continuity and coherence to the coaching relationship.

In our work with school districts, coaching hundreds of principals and assistant principals, we have identified some best practices or strategies that have been very successful. We recommend that the coaching plan includes a principal or assistant principal assessment to determine some baseline information Using an Emotional Intelligence Survey, Equity Leadership Dispositions Questionnaire (Leadership Academy, 2020), and Strengths Finder (Rath, 2007) can also be very informative in getting to know the coachee's strengths. For example, a coach can be more effective in developing the coachee's skills and knowledge when building on the coachee's previous experiences. For example, if the coaching session is focused on supporting students who are struggling with

FIGURE 14.3 ● Collaborative Log

COLLABORATIVE LOG

CANDIDATE: _____ DATE: _____

MENTOR: _____ SCHOOL: _____

☐ What's Working?	☐ Current Focus, Challenges, Concerns
☐ Coachee's Next Steps	☐ Coach's Next Steps
☐ Next Meeting Date	☐ Next Meeting Agenda

- Facilitating a Vision of Learning
- Shaping the School Culture and Instructional Program
- Managing the Organization

- Collaborating with Families and Communities
- Modeling Ethics and Building Leadership Capacity
- Responding to the Political, Social, Economic, Legal & Cultural Context

NEW TEACHER CENTER @ UCSC; used with permission.

Source: Reprinted with permission from the New Teacher Center, https://newteachercenter.org

reading grade-level materials, then it is helpful to the coach to know that the principal they are coaching was a former reading teacher. That knowledge will help the coach target questions knowing the principal has knowledge of diagnostic techniques and assessments, reading strategies, and instructional interventions. Reviewing the district's performance evaluation or goal setting documents is important if the goal of coaching is to align coaching to the professional growth plan established by the principal supervisor. Reviewing school and student data in collaboration with the principal or assistant principal is helpful to both the coach and coachee. It is an excellent way to determine the priorities of the principal, to better understand the context in which he or she works, and to learn more about the teaching staff, students, and programs in place at the school. The diagram below provides an example of a coaching plan that has been aligned to the three skill areas and six behaviors that have been identified as effective practices by research (Grissom, Egalite, & Lindsay, 2021). The coach can use the IDP to determine priorities for the principal that have the greatest impact on student achievement. The IDP recommends using assessment tools to gather information that will provide the coach with information that can inform coaching discussions. But focusing coaching sessions on skill areas that have been found in the research literature to lead to improved student learning in reading and math should be a priority (Figure 14.4).

FIGURE 14.4 ● Developing a Coaching Plan

Coaching Plan

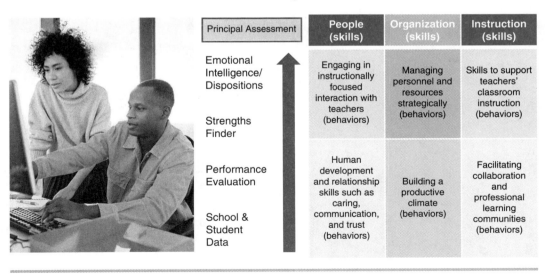

Principal Assessment	People (skills)	Organization (skills)	Instruction (skills)
Emotional Intelligence/ Dispositions Strengths Finder	Engaging in instructionally focused interaction with teachers (behaviors)	Managing personnel and resources strategically (behaviors)	Skills to support teachers' classroom instruction (behaviors)
Performance Evaluation School & Student Data	Human development and relationship skills such as caring, communication, and trust (behaviors)	Building a productive climate (behaviors)	Facilitating collaboration and professional learning communities (behaviors)

Photo credit: iStock.com/xavierarnau

Principals make lots of decisions each day that have implications for the professional growth and success of teachers and support staff. Grissom, Egalite, and Lindsay (2021) found in their study *How Principals Affect Students and Schools: A Systematic Synthesis of Two Decades or Research* that three skills really matter to the effectiveness of principal leadership. The three areas include skill working with people, the organization, and instruction. The authors identified specific skills such as engaging in instructionally focused interactions with teachers (people) and building a productive climate (organization) and facilitating collaboration and professional learning communities (instruction). As the coach begin their work with a principal, assistant principal, or teacher, it is very important to have a plan informed by evidence and targeted to the coachee's professional growth priorities.

Reflection: As a coach what are some initial steps that you will take to assure that you have the information you need to support your coachee? As a coachee, what information is important for you to share with your coach?

CHAPTER 15

Case Study Long Beach Unified and Delaware Academy for School Leadership

BUILDING A CULTURE OF COACHING AT LOCAL AND STATE LEVELS: TWO CASE STUDIES

Long Beach Unified School District is in Long Beach, California. The district educates 65,000 students in 84 public schools in the cities of Long Beach, Lakewood, Signal Hill, and Avalon on Catalina Island. The school district is the fourth largest in California and serves one of the most diverse large cities in the United States. The student population is 59.1% Hispanic, 12.4% African American, 12.1% white, 6.7% Asian, 5.5% multirace, 1.1% Pacific Islander, and 2.8% Filipino. The district serves 15.1% English language learners and 64.3% of the students are economically disadvantaged. The school district employs more than 10,000 people.

Long Beach Unified School District has earned a national reputation as one of America's finest school systems, winning many awards as a national and international model of excellence. The Global Education Study by the nonprofit Battelle for

Kids organization lists the LBUSD among five of the world's highest performing school systems. The McKinsey & Company, in a comprehensive analysis of global school system reform, ranked LBUSD as one of the world's top improving school systems in the United States in terms of sustained and significant improvements.

But what is the "secret sauce" that leads to Long Beach Unified School District's continuous improvement and student success? If you ask Superintendent Dr. Jill Baker, you will get the same answer every time, *We invest in our people*. The district has spent more than a decade building programs for teacher leaders, aspiring administrators, principals, and central office leaders. Individuals are identified, tapped, and encouraged to participate in job embedded professional growth opportunities. The district has also designed leadership development programs for educators that provide a career pathway for teacher leaders, instructional specialists, mentors, assistant principals, principals, principal supervisors, and other district personnel positions. Dr. Kelly An serves as the Director of Equity, Leadership and Talent Development. In this role, she plans and facilitates a comprehensive leadership development program that provides opportunities for educators to receive professional development and coaching to improve their leadership knowledge and skills.

According to Dr. Baker, the district leadership team collaborated to determine the instructional needs of school leaders in the Long Beach Unified School District. This work and the district's approach has been affirmed by the research from RAND, conducted as part of the Wallace Foundation Principal Pipeline Initiative. One of the findings in the RAND report was that formal programs, for growing new principals, are a cost-effective method of improving student performance and contributing to principal retention. In studying 12 district leadership pipeline programs, RAND found professional coaching to be a successful method of building the mindset and improving the performance of administrators.

LBUSD's focus on coaching began with support for new principals. Initial leadership development programming began with a single central office administrator conducting a coaching program for new principals offering "just in time" support during their first two years on the job. Due to the success of the initial coaching support, the district began training current principals in coaching methodology to use to coach new principals. Principal to principal coaching was central to capacity building for site administrators. Over time, the coaching expanded to central office administrators, principal supervisors, principals coaching assistant principals, and principals and assistant principals coaching teachers. Coaching as a way of being in LBUSD means that everyone in the district is continually improved by being coached. There is a *culture of coaching* throughout the entire system where the growth, development, and support of all employees is valued and prioritized. There is a belief that coaching supports reflective practice, relationship building, and personal development in the service to students.

The Long Beach Unified School District has invested in training and practice. One key coaching model used in the LBUSD is *Blended Coaching*. In the fall and spring coaches attend professional development focused on problems of practice using a triad model of coaching. Triad coaching provides an opportunity to practice questioning techniques such as consultative, collaborative, transformational, and facilitative processes. By role-playing in triads, coaches can practice their coaching skills and receive feedback from colleagues. There is always a discussion about next steps as coaches improve their coaching skills. A foundational tenet of coaching is that it is not a one-size-fits-all process. The strategies depend on the needs of the individual being coached. Often coaches move between instructional and facilitative coaching, strategically shifting between the two approaches.

Long Beach Unified School District is intentional about relationship building and the coaching partnerships. One strategy implemented in Long Beach has been a Principal Supervisor Lab Day. Several times a year, principal supervisors visit schools as a group and observe classroom instruction. The visit is followed by the principal coaching a teacher while others observe and provide feedback to the principal. Next to be observed is the principal supervisor coaching the principal around the teacher conference. Everyone is coached and everyone is learning and improving their skills and knowledge to better serve students. Professional practice is public, and is centered around nurturing growth.

In the small state of Delaware, coaching has become a primary strategy to support and grow the principal pipeline. During the United States Department of Education federal funding of Race to the Top, the Delaware Department of Education Educator Effectiveness Unit leadership team identified coaching as a strategy to help principals provide formative feedback to teachers using the state performance evaluation system. The Delaware Academy for School Leadership

(DASL), a professional development, policy, and research center in the College of Education and Human Development at the University of Delaware, was selected to provide coaching support throughout the state to over 150 principals.

Experienced administrators who had been principals, super-intendents, and curriculum directors were hired and trained as Leadership Specialists using a model of blended coaching. At that time, several coaching models were considered, but the Blended Coaching model was determined to be the best fit for the work because it focused on ways of doing and ways of being with the ability to shift from facilitative coaching to instructional coaching when needed. Coaches accompanied the principals during classroom observations, used facilitative coaching strategies to determine what principals observed, what data they collected during the lesson, and the formative feedback they planned to provide to teachers during the post conference. Coaches often used role-playing with principals to practice postobservation meetings with teachers.

The "Development Coaches," as they were formally named, supported principals with the implementation of the new performance evaluation system through facilitative conversations about what they observed, what feedback they should provide to the teacher, and resources that might be useful to improve the pedagogical knowledge of the teacher. If the principal did not have the expertise, they needed to provide feedback to the teacher in a particular area, the coach used instructional coaching to provide resources, ideas, and strategies to grow the coachee's skills and knowledge.

The DEDOE has continued to partner with the Delaware Academy for School Leadership to provide coaching support to novice assistant principals and principals in high needs schools. School districts have also requested coaching support for novice principals or principals who need additional support. Coaching-based support is now embedded in virtually all Delaware schools, funded by the state.

Conclusion

Sometimes we don't know what we don't know. I didn't think I needed support but you have helped me be more reflective and intentional about my decisions.
—Middle School Principal

When my supervisor told me that I would be assigned a leadership coach, I thought she was saying that I was not doing a good job. When I told her how I felt, she told me it was just the opposite of what I thought. She saw great potential in me and thought a leadership coach would provide me with a great professional growth experience.
—Elementary Assistant Principal

I really think I am making a difference here, and you have helped me to make that difference.
—High School Principal

I had no idea what I was getting into; I wouldn't have made it without you.
—Principal K-8 Charter School

I want a coach for the rest of my career. This is the way I learn!
—5th grade math teacher

These are just a few of the representative comments we've heard from the many individuals we've had the privilege of supporting through coaching. Our daily work as coaches and supervisors offers us the opportunity to interact with some of the most dedicated, passionate, and hard-working people on the planet. They do some of the toughest and most important work imaginable.

However, it is unfortunately true that many do not have access to professional coaching or Coaching-Based Supervision. Some individuals are able to succeed in what has been an isolated, sink-or-swim profession despite weak preservice and inservice professional development. Others, by accident or by design, cobble together a functional support system.

Our experience tells us that the work of coaching K-12 professionals is not easy. It is both risky and complex, but it is worth the investment in energy and commitment, in time and training.

Research suggests that coaching supports collective leadership across a school system (Annenberg Foundation for Education Reform, 2004). An essential feature of coaching is that it uses the relationships between coaches, principals, and teachers to create the conversation that leads to behavioral, pedagogical, and content knowledge change. Effective coaching distributes leadership and keeps the focus on teaching and learning. This focus promotes the development of leadership skills, professional learning, and support for teachers that target ways to improve student outcomes. In this book we have laid the groundwork for the establishment of what we believe is a distinct professional niche in the education community. Coaching is making a difference for our schools, our kids, and our society. We welcome you to this important work, and we invite you to join us in what we hope will be a vibrant learning community of committed and professional coaches.

Leadership Coaching Resources

The additional resource materials in this section are organized into four sections, as follows:

A. **Materials for Coach Professional Development**

A.1 **Bias Worksheet**. This worksheet is a self-reflection tool for coaches and others. It is intended to help you understand how your experiences and perspectives impact the way you perceive and behave in the world and how they might affect your coaching practice.

A.2 **Assessments Self-Reflection**. In Chapter 4, we introduced the distinction between assertions and assessments and the notion that poorly formed assessments can limit our possibilities. This self-reflection is designed to help coaches and others examine the assessments they make about themselves.

A.3 **Coaching Feedback**. This is one example of the kind of simple tool that should be used by coaches and coaching programs to solicit feedback from coachees in order to strengthen the continual improvement processes of both coaches and programs.

A.4 **Ethics for Coaches**. This document outlines ethical standards for coaching practice.

A.5 **Principal Supervisor Self-Assessment**. This is an excerpt from Coaching-Based Supervision for Principal Supervisors which may serve as a template for the development of role-based self-assessments. This document is based upon the Council of Chief State School Officers Standards for Principal Supervisors.

B. **Establishing the Coaching Relationship**

B.1 **Making the Most of the Coaching Relationship**. This handout lets new coachees know what to expect and encourages them to invest in the coaching relationship.

Consider sharing this document with coachees and their supervisors.

B.2 **Coaching Agreement**. This is a sample contract between coach and coachee, outlining the responsibilities of each party. We suggest that this document or one like it be discussed and signed early in the coaching relationship.

C. **Formative Assessment Tools**

C.1 **Standards-Based Assessment**. A coachee, coach, and supervisor can use this sort of tool to assess a coachee's strengths and needs in relation to standards. This can be used as a formative tool—for the purpose of informing the creation of a professional development plan such as the Individual Development Plan that follows—and as a summative assessment.

C.2 **Dispositions Self-Assessment**. Coaches and coachees may want to use this self-assessment as a tool for reflecting upon their personal beliefs in relation to the dispositions called for in the PSEL Standards, from which it is derived.

C.3 **360° Survey**. Surveys such as this 360° instrument are immensely valuable to coaches and coachees for gathering perceptual data. We recommend that all leaders use a 360° instrument annually and that leadership coaches use the instrument as a primary source for determining the focus of the coaching process.

C.4 **Individual Development Plan (IDP)**. This is a template for an annual professional development plan tied to the PSEL Standards. In a coherent coaching-based professional development program, such a plan guides coaching and other professional development activities and is tied to the district's evaluation system.

C.5 **Collaborative Log**. We suggest that this Collaborative Log serve as an organizer and a record for each coaching session. It is completed collaboratively, and both the coach and coachee keep copies.

D. **Support for Coaching-Based Supervision**

D.1 **Developing a Coaching Supervision Strategy**. This worksheet is designed to help supervisors plan an overall, medium-term approach to supervision. Reviewing a supervisee's prior evaluations, needs, and goals, how will you proceed?

D.2 **Coaching/Supervision Session Plan**. This form is designed to guide the planning and evaluation of a coaching session. Great coaches and supervisors develop the habits of mind reflected in this planning document.

D.3 **Coaching/Supervision Log**. A sample meeting log for coaching-based supervision.

D.4 **Planning for Supervisorial Feedback and Direction (PD & I)**. This tool is designed to help a supervisor think through the process of providing feedback and/or direction to a supervisee.

D.5 **Classroom Observation Template**. A notetaking and discussion guide for principal supervisors, principals, and others conducting classroom visitations.

D.6 **Some Coaching and Coaching-Based Supervision Language Stems**. These language stems sum up the essential moves of Blended Coaching and Coaching-Based Supervision. Some of our colleagues have laminated this sheet and use it as a daily source of guidance.

RESOURCE A: MATERIALS FOR COACH PROFESSIONAL DEVELOPMENT

A.1. BIAS WORKSHEET

This worksheet is a self-reflection tool for coaches and others. It is intended to help you understand how your experiences and perspectives impact the way you perceive and behave in the world and how they might affect your coaching practice.

What are the key factors of your personal background that shape the way you see the world?

Gender Identity	Family Background
Culture	**Professional Experience**
Personal Style	Race/Ethnicity

A.2. ASSESSMENTS SELF-REFLECTION

In Chapter 4 we introduced the distinction between assertions and assessments and the notion that poorly formed assessments can limit our possibilities. This self-reflection is designed to help coaches and others examine the assessments they make about themselves.

1. Quickly brainstorm words that describe positive (+) or negative (−) assessments you make about yourself:

(+) Assessment	(−) Assessment

2. Circle one of the positive assessments you wrote above. What assertions can you make to ground that assessment? What narratives are built around that assessment?

3. Circle one negative assessment. What assertions can you make to ground that assessment? What narratives are built around that assessment?

4. What assertions can you make that do not support the negative assessment?

5. What different assessments and narratives would open more possibilities for you?

A.3. COACHING FEEDBACK

This is one example of the kind of simple tool that should be used by coaches and coaching programs to solicit feedback from coachees in order to strengthen the continual improvement processes of both coaches and programs.

Feedback for Coaches

To:_____   Date:_____

In what areas of your professional work are you feeling most successful?	What are your greatest concerns and challenges?
What coaching strategies do I use that are most helpful to you?	What additional ideas or suggestions do you have to help me be a better coach?

A.4. ETHICS FOR COACHES

This document outlines ethical standards for coaching practice.

Code of Ethics for Coaches

- I will conduct myself in a manner that serves the goal of doing what is bestfor students.

- I will coach my client with the goal of supporting the development of performance aligned with accepted professional standards.

- I will build trust in my coaching relationships by consistently being sincere in my communication, reliable in meeting my commitments, and by operating within my areas of competence.

- I will, at the beginning of each coaching relationship, ensure that my client understands the terms of the coaching agreement between us.

- I will respect the confidentiality of my client's information, except as otherwise authorized by my client, or as required by law.

- I will coordinate with and support the goals of my client's employer, while guarding confidentiality and nurturing collaboration between all parties.

- I will be alert to noticing when my client is no longer benefiting from our coaching relationship and thus would be better served by another coach or by another resource and, at that time, I will encourage my client to make that change.

- I will avoid conflicts between my interests and the interests of my clients. Whenever the potential for a conflict of interest arises, I will discuss the conflict with my client to reach agreement with my client on how to deal with it in whatever way best serves my client.

A.5. PRINCIPAL SUPERVISOR SELF-ASSESSMENT

STANDARD 2: Principal Supervisors coach and support individual principles and engage in effective professional learning strategies to help principals grow as instructional leaders.[1]

Questions to reflect upon:
• Do I see myself as "the boss" or as a facilitator and coach? How do others see me?
• How do I build capacity by coaching rather than by directing and telling?
• When appropriate, have I given supervisorial feedback and direction?
• Are we having difficult conversations and working from a sense of urgency in relation to student achievement?
• How do I balance the need to support my principals with day-to-day and operational problems against the need to focus upon ongoing instructional improvement?
• Do I manage my supervisorial relationships by maintaining a focus upon shared goals and holding myself and my principals accountable for follow-through from meeting to meeting?
• How well is our principal team functioning as a professional learning community? Do we spend our time together focused upon teaching and learning?

Evidence of my effective practice:

Areas for my growth:

Goals:	Next step(s):

---

[1]The Sample Self-Assessment for Principal Supervisors was developed for and used by six school districts participating in The Wallace Foundation's Principal Supervisor Initiative, which ran from 2014–2018. This tool has not been formally reviewed or endorsed by the foundation.

RESOURCE B: ESTABLISHING THE COACHING RELATIONSHIP

B.1. MAKING THE MOST OF THE COACHING RELATIONSHIP

This handout lets new coachees know what to expect and encourages them to invest in the coaching relationship. Consider sharing this document with coachees and their supervisors.

MAKING THE MOST OF COACHING

Masterful coaches inspire people by helping them recognize the previously unseen possibilities that lay embedded in their existing circumstances.

—Robert Hargrove, *author of* Masterful Coaching

The purpose of this document is to provide you with some basic information that will help you make the most of coaching. If you have additional questions, be sure to share them with your coach.

What is professional coaching? Coaching is a one-to-one process for the purpose of helping you clarify your professional goals and achieve them. The ultimate goal of the process is to have a positive impact upon student achievement. Your coach will use a variety of strategies to support your learning. At times your coach will play an *instructional* role, serving as a personal teacher, consultant, and collaborator. Often, your coach will take what we call a *facilitative* approach, stimulating your learning through questioning, by providing you with feedback, helping you to analyze your perceptions and behaviors, and guiding you as you experiment with new ways of doing things. Unlike many other professional development models, your coach is there to meet your individual needs.

What kinds of things will we do in coaching? You and your coach will meet regularly, and every session will differ. Much of your time will be spent in conversation, but it is also important that your coach has the opportunity to observe you interacting with people at your site and doing real work. You and your coach may also decide to use survey instruments and other data sources to gather feedback and information to use in the coaching process.

Are these sessions confidential? Your work may be highly sensitive, demanding, and political, and confidentiality is critical to the success of coaching. Your coach's commitment is to confidentiality. Aside from sharing general descriptions of the type of work you are doing, your coach will not discuss your coaching relationship with anyone, including your supervisor, without your agreement.

Is coaching a remedial process? Absolutely not. Top athletes, business leaders, and school leaders take advantage of coaching as an important tool for professional growth. Teachers appreciate that principals participating in coaching are modeling lifelong learning for their staff.

How can I make the most of coaching? Coaching is not a passive process, and the benefits you gain from coaching will be influenced by the degree to which you take advantage of the process. Here are some of the most important things you can do to make the most of coaching:

- Build uninterrupted time into your schedule for coaching.
- Take initiative in asking your coach to observe you in difficult situations.
- Be forthcoming about your problems, doubts, and toughest issues. Let it all hang out.
- Be willing to take risks with your coach in dealing with uncomfortable topics and in experimenting with uncomfortable solutions.
- Between coaching sessions, keep track of goals and action plans you have established with your coach.
- Between coaching sessions, note issues and concerns that might be fruitful to discuss with your coach.
- Be forthcoming with your coach about anything your coach is doing that is interfering with your ability to get the most out of the relationship.

Congratulations and thanks for taking on some of the most important work in the world.

B.2. COACHING AGREEMENT

This is a sample contract between coach and coachee, outlining the responsibilities of each party. We suggest that this document or one like it be discussed and signed early in the coaching relationship.

Sample Coaching Agreement

Coach agrees

- To honor the confidentiality of work with Participant

- To provide one-on-one support to Participant for a minimum of 3 hours per month

- To utilize proven coaching approaches in work with Participant

- To serve as a support to Participant when possible by securing information, contacts, and other resources as requested and as appropriate

- To respond to Participant in a timely manner between coaching sessions via telephone or e-mail

- To honor the demanding schedule of site administrators, offering services on site whenever possible and avoiding duplication of programs and commitments

- To convene and facilitate occasional job-alike and topical gatherings of program participants

- To commit to supporting the success and effectiveness of Participant as the primary focus and purpose of the program

Participant agrees

- To fully avail him/herself of the support offered by the Coach

- To work with the Coach to identify meaningful goals for the program, in concert with the development of individual goals as required by the Participant's school district

- To approach the coaching relationship with openness and honesty

- To arrange for observations of real-work situations that will allow for targeted coaching, such as:

  - A teacher observation cycle

  - Development of a teacher development case study

  - Facilitation of a staff or site council meeting

- To participate in the evaluation of the program and to contribute ideas to the design and revision of the program
- To take full advantage of written materials and other resources made available by the program
- To participate in three off-site meetings during the course of the school year

Participant: _____

Coach: _____

Date: _____

RESOURCE C: FORMATIVE ASSESSMENT TOOLS

C.1. STANDARDS-BASED ASSESSMENT

A coachee, coach, and supervisor can use this sort of tool to assess a coachee's strengths and needs in relation to standards. This can be used as a formative tool—for the purpose of informing the creation of a professional development plan such as the Individual Development Plan that follows—and as a summative assessment.

Self-Assessment of Skills in Relation to the Professional Standards for Educational Leaders (PSEL)

STANDARD	WHAT SUCCESSES HAVE YOU EXPERIENCED THIS YEAR?	WHAT CHALLENGES DO YOU STILL FACE?	WHAT PROFESSIONAL DEVELOPMENT DO YOU NEED?
St. 1 Mission, Vision, and Core Values Effective educational leaders develop, advocate, and enact a shared mission, vision, and core values of high-quality education and academic success and well-being of each student			
St. 2 Ethics and Professional Norms Effective educational leaders act ethically and according to professional norms to promote each student's academic success and well-being.			

(Continued)

(Continued)

STANDARD	WHAT SUCCESSES HAVE YOU EXPERIENCED THIS YEAR?	WHAT CHALLENGES DO YOU STILL FACE?	WHAT PROFESSIONAL DEVELOPMENT DO YOU NEED?
St. 3 Equity and Cultural Responsiveness Effective educational leaders strive for equity of educational opportunity and culturally responsive practices to promote each student's academic success and well-being.			
St. 4 Curriculum, Instruction, and Assessment Effective educational leaders develop and support intellectually rigorous and coherent systems of curriculum, instruction, and assessment to promote each student's academic success and well-being.			
St. 5 Community of Care and Support for Students Effective educational leaders cultivate an inclusive, caring, and supportive school community that promotes the academic success and well-being of each student.			

(Continued)

STANDARD	WHAT SUCCESSES HAVE YOU EXPERIENCED THIS YEAR?	WHAT CHALLENGES DO YOU STILL FACE?	WHAT PROFESSIONAL DEVELOPMENT DO YOU NEED?
St. 6 Professional Capacity of School Personnel Effective educational leaders develop the professional capacity and practice of school personnel to promote each student's academic success and well-being.			
St. 7 Professional Community for Teachers and Staff Effective educational leaders foster a professional community of teachers and other professional staff to promote each student's academic success and well-being.			
St. 8 Meaningful Engagement of Families and Communities Effective educational leaders foster a professional community of teachers and other professional staff to promote each student's academic success and well-being.			

(Continued)

(Continued)

STANDARD	WHAT SUCCESSES HAVE YOU EXPERIENCED THIS YEAR?	WHAT CHALLENGES DO YOU STILL FACE?	WHAT PROFESSIONAL DEVELOPMENT DO YOU NEED?
St. 9 Operations and Management Effective educational leaders manage school operations and resources to promote each student's academic success and well-being.			
St. 10 School Improvement Effective educational leaders act as agents of continuous improvement to promote each student's academic success and well-being.			

C.2. DISPOSITIONS SELF-ASSESSMENT

Coaches and coachees may want to use this self-assessment as a tool for reflecting upon their personal beliefs and dispositions

Dispositions Self-Assessment

TO WHAT DEGREE DO YOU BELIEVE IN, VALUE, AND COMMIT YOURSELF TO ...	NOT AT ALL	SOMEWHAT	MIND, HEART, AND SOUL
Student learning as the fundamental purpose of schooling			
The ideal of the common good and the principles of the Bill of Rights			
The right of every student to a free, quality education			
Working tirelessly to insure that schools produce equitable outcomes			
Using the influence of one's office with ethics and integrity in the service of all students and their families			
A safe and supportive learning environment			
The proposition that all students can learn			
A school vision of high standards and expectations of learning			
Continuous school improvement			
The proposition that diversity enriches the school			
Collaboration and communication with families, community, students, and other			

(Continued)

TO WHAT DEGREE DO YOU BELIEVE IN, VALUE, AND COMMIT YOURSELF TO ...	NOT AT ALL	SOMEWHAT	MIND, HEART, AND SOUL
stakeholder groups and their involvement in decision-making			
Ensuring that students have the knowledge, skills, and values needed to become successful adults			
A willingness to continuously examine one's own assumptions, innate prejudices, beliefs, and practices			
Doing the work and taking the responsibility required for high levels of personal and organizational performance			
Lifelong learning for self and others			
Professional development as an integral part of school improvement			
The proposition that families have the best interests of their children in mind			
Preparing students to become contributing members of society			
Taking risks to improve schools			
Trusting people and their judgments and involving them in leadership and management processes			
Actively participating in the political and policymaking context in the service of education			

C.3. 360° SURVEY

Surveys such as this 360° instrument are immensely valuable to coaches and coachees for gathering perceptual data. We recommend that all leaders use a 360° instrument annually and that leadership coaches use the instrument as a primary source for determining the focus of the coaching process.

Sample 360° Leadership Survey

Name of Principal: _____

Your role: _____

Please rate the principal's effectiveness in each area by placing an **X** along the continuum of development from **Beginning** to **Accomplished**. Your specific comments and suggestions will be particularly helpful.

←——— **Beginning** ————————————————— **Accomplished** ———→
ENSURES THE SAFE, EFFICIENT, AND EFFECTIVE MANAGEMENT OF THE SCHOOL
(Sustains a safe, well-maintained learning environment for students and staff)
(Effectively manages student discipline policies and procedures)
(Provides the necessary resources to support the learning of all students)
COMMENTS and/or SUGGESTIONS

(Continued)

(Continued)

Beginning	Accomplished

FACILITATES THE DEVELOPMENT OF A VISION OF LEARNING THAT IS SHARED AND SUPPORTED BY THE SCHOOL COMMUNITY

(Promotes a vision of student achievement based upon data from multiple measures of student learning)

(Shapes and coordinates school programs to ensure they are well communicated and consistent with the vision)

(Effectively builds buy-in within the entire school community)

COMMENTS and/or SUGGESTIONS

Beginning   Accomplished

←――――――――――――――――――――――――――――――→

BUILDS AND SUSTAINS A SCHOOL CULTURE AND INSTRUCTIONAL PROGRAM CONDUCIVE TO STUDENT LEARNING AND STAFF PROFESSIONAL GROWTH

(Promotes equity, fairness, and respect among all members of the school community)

(Shapes a culture of high expectations, built upon a system of standards-based accountability)

(Provides opportunities for all members of the school community to collaborate, share responsibility, and exercise leadership)

COMMENTS and/or SUGGESTIONS

(Continued)

(Continued)

Beginning	Accomplished

BUILDS AND SUSTAINS A SCHOOL CULTURE AND INSTRUCTIONAL PROGRAM CONDUCIVE TO STUDENT LEARNING AND STAFF PROFESSIONAL GROWTH

(Promotes equity, fairness, and respect among all members of the school community)

(Shapes a culture of high expectations, built upon a system of standards-based accountability)

(Provides opportunities for all members of the school community to collaborate, share responsibility, and exercise leadership)

COMMENTS and/or SUGGESTIONS

Beginning	Accomplished

MODELS EFFECTIVE PROFESSIONAL LEADERSHIP, INTERPERSONAL SKILLS, ETHICS, AND INTEGRITY

(Demonstrates skills in decision-making, problem-solving, change management, conflict resolution, planning, and evaluation)

(Encourages and inspires others to higher levels of performance and motivation)

(Builds and maintains effective interpersonal relationships)

(Demonstrates knowledge of curriculum and ability to be an instructional leader)

(Models personal and professional ethics, integrity, and fairness)

COMMENTS and/or SUGGESTIONS

(Continued)

(Continued)

Beginning	Accomplished

UNDERSTANDS AND ENGAGES WITH IMPORTANT ISSUES BEYOND THE SITE LEVEL

(Works with central office and the school board to influence policies that benefit students)

(Ensures that the school complies with federal, state, and district requirements)

(Views him/herself as a leader of a team and as a member of a larger team)

COMMENTS and/or SUGGESTIONS

C.4. INDIVIDUAL DEVELOPMENT PLAN (IDP)

This is a template for an annual professional development plan. In a coherent coaching-based professional development program, such a plan guides coaching and other professional development activities and is tied to the district's evaluation system.

INDIVIDUALIZED DEVELOPMENT PLAN (IDP)

STANDARD: _____

COACHEE _____

COACH _____

ELEMENT OF THE STANDARD: _____

SUPERVISOR _____

ACTIVITIES	PERSONS RESPONSIBLE	TIMELINE JUL AUG SEPT OCT NOV DEC JAN FEB MAR APR MAY JUN	EVALUATION	DATE OF REFLECTION INQUIRY MEETING

I approve and will support the implementation of the IDP.

COACHEE _____ Date _____

COACH _____ Date _____

SUPERVISOR _____ Date _____

Source: Reprinted with permission from the New Teacher Center, https://newteachercenter.org

C.5. COLLABORATIVE LOG

We suggest that this Collaborative Log serve as an organizer and a record for each coaching session. It is completed collaboratively, and both the coach and coachee keep copies.

Candidate: _____   Date: _____

Mentor: _____   School: _____

What's Working?	Current Focus, Challenges, Concerns
Coachee's Next Steps	Coach's Next Steps
Next Meeting Date	Next Meeting Agenda

RESOURCE D: SUPPORT FOR COACHING-BASED SUPERVISION

D.1. DEVELOPING A COACHING SUPERVISION STRATEGY (PD & I)[2]

This worksheet is designed as a tool to help supervisors plan an overall, medium-term approach to supervision. In reviewing a supervisee's prior evaluation, current needs, and goals, how will you proceed?

Key desired outcomes:
Relevant background factors:
What do you hope to learn, and what do you hope to develop through facilitative coaching?
Key meditational questions:
What supervisorial feedback and direction might you need to provide?
What technical knowledge and capacity does the principal need? What instructional, collaborative, and consultative coaching and support might you provide?
Does the principal need to develop core dispositions, leadership style, emotional intelligence, relationship skills, or other ways of being in order to meet the outcomes? If so, how will you support this growth through transformational coaching?

---

[2]Developing a Coaching Supervision Strategy was developed for and used by six school districts participating in The Wallace Foundation' Principal Supervisor Initiative, which ran from 2014–2018. This tool has not been formally reviewed or endorsed by the foundation.

D.2. COACHING/SUPERVISION SESSION PLAN[3]

Supervisor: _____   Principal: _____

Date: _____   Site: _____

Your top four goals in working with this principal/site linked to school and principal evaluation goals and data points: 1. 2. 3. 4.	
Progress to date	**Concerns**

Check in on Prior Commitments/Follow Up

Supervisor	Principal
If observing classrooms or other activity this visit, what are you looking for?	
Goals/outcomes for today's sessions	
Potential coaching strategies/questions • Facilitative • Instructional • Transformational	
Potential supervisorial feedback	
Potential supervisorial direction	

Possible Next Steps

Supervisor	Principal

---

[3]The Coaching/Supervision Session Plan was developed for and used by six school districts participating in The Wallace Foundation's Principal Supervisor Initiative, which ran from 2014–2018. This tool has not been formally reviewed or endorsed by the foundation.

Post-Supervision/Coaching Reflection

To what extent did I achieve my planned outcomes?
How did I apply coaching strategies, and what worked? What didn't?
Did I provide supervisorial feedback and/or direction? If so, was it appropriate and well received?
What did I learn about the principal and or/the site through conversation and/or observation?
What impact did this session have upon the principal?
What will serve as evidence of principal growth in response to this and related sessions?
How will our experience with this session shape my planning for and conduct of our next session?

D.3. COACHING/SUPERVISION LOG[4]

Supervisor: _____   Principal: _____

Date: _____   Site: _____

Planned focus and outcomes for this session	
What's working?	Opportunities for growth

Follow-Up From Prior Meetings

Supervisor	Principal
Through observations and/or other data gathering, what did you learn today?	
What are the implications of today's session and linkages to site and personal goals?	

Next Steps and Due Dates

Supervisor	Principal
Next Meeting	

---

[4]The Coaching/Supervisior Log was developed for and used by six school districts participating in The Wallace Foundation's Principal Supervisor Initiative, which ran from 2014–2018. This tool has not been formally reviewed or endorsed by the foundation.

D.4. PLANNING FOR SUPERVISORIAL FEEDBACK AND DIRECTION (PD & I)[5]

This tool is designed to help a supervisor think through the process of providing feedback and/or direction to a supervisee.

What is your concern?
What evidence do you have to support that concern?
How does this link to explicit goals, standards, expectations, and teaching and learning?
What relevant history or other factors are related to this concern?
When and how can you provide this feedback in a way that is likely to be received productively?
What do you want as the outcome(s) of this conversation?
Outline the statements you will make in sharing this feedback with the principal.
How will you provide specific direction to the principal and/or coach him/her to commit to an action plan and next steps?
What feedback do you hope to get from the principal on your role in the conversation?
What do you expect to be your next steps coming out of the conversation?

---

[5]Planning for Supervisorial Feedback and Direction was developed for and used by six school districts participating in The Wallace Foundation's Principal Supervisor Initiative, which ran from 2014–2018. This tool has not been formally reviewed or endorsed by the foundation.

D.5. CLASSROOM OBSERVATION TEMPLATE[6]

School/Principal: _____   Date: _____

Today's "looks-fors"

Teacher	Subject
Teacher Actions	Student Actions

Evidence of Learning	Wonderings	Next Steps

Teacher	Subject
Teacher Actions	Student Actions

Evidence of Learning	Wonderings	Next Steps

Teacher	Subject
Teacher Actions	Student Actions

Evidence of Learning	Wonderings	Next Steps

Our "big picture" Take-Aways, Next Steps, and Actionable Feedback

---

[6]The Classroom Observation Template was developed for and used by six school districts participating in The Wallace Foundation's Principal Supervisor Initiative, which ran from 2014–2018. This tool has not been formally reviewed or endorsed by the foundation.

D.6. SOME COACHING AND COACHING-BASED SUPERVISION LANGUAGE STEMS

OPENING

- What do we hope to achieve in our meeting today?
- In following up from last week, this is what we agreed to work on...
- Tell me about your progress in relation to...

PARAPHRASING

- So you are saying that...
- I am hearing that...
- You are noticing that...

PROBING PARAPHRASE

- You are telling me that (with added specificity)...
- I hear that you have two concerns...
- In other words (with added clarity)...

CLARIFYING QUESTIONS

- Tell me more about...
- What do you mean by "my teachers"?
- What does low achievement mean to you?

MEDIATIONAL QUESTIONS

- What would it look like if...?
- What would be the arguments against...?
- Can you imagine another way to...?

INSTRUCTIONAL COACHING

- Can I share some information about...?
- What I saw in classrooms is...
- Research on best practice indicates...

CONSULTATIVE COACHING

- Here are two options you might consider...
- I can bring these resources to you...
- The data tell me that...

COLLABORATIVE COACHING

- Let's look at the data together...
- We can work together to...
- Can I play a supportive role by...?

SUPERVISORIAL FEEDBACK

- I have rated you as "developing" based on this evidence...
- This is how I and others experience your communication style...
- I have total confidence in your ability to...

SUPERVISORIAL DIRECTION

- I expect you to... by...
- Please share your plan to...
- You'll need to... in order to...

TRANSFORMATIONAL COACHING

- Let's role-play...
- Practice doing...
- What might be another narrative you could tell yourself?

SUMMARIZING

- Let's review our next steps...
- We'll know that we have achieved our goals when...

References

Anderson, J. (March 31, 2013). Curious grade for teachers: Nearly all pass. *The New York Times*, A1.

Annenberg Foundation for Education Reform. (2004). *Professional development strategies that improve instruction*.

Austin, S. (April 1, 2015). *4 steps of inquiry that help principals improve instruction*. Retrieved from https://k-12leadership.org/4-steps-of-inquiry-that-help-principals-improve-instruction/

Bickman, L., Goldring, E., DeAndrade, A. R., Breda, C., & Goff, P. (March 8–10, 2012). Improving principal leadership through feedback and coaching. *Paper presented at the annual meeting of the society for research on educational effectiveness*. Washington, DC.

Block, P. (2000). *Flawless consulting*. San Francisco, CA: Jossey-Bass.

Borko, H., Liston, D., & Whitcomb, J. (2007). Apples and fishes: The debate over dispositions in teacher education. *Journal of Teacher Education, 58*(5), 359–364.

Brooks, M. (1989). *Instant rapport*. New York, NY: Warner Books.

Brounstein, M. (2000). *Coaching and mentoring for dummies*. Foster City, CA: IDG Books.

Brown, B. (2021). *Atlas of the heart: Mapping meaningful connection and the language of human experience*. New York, NY: Random House.

Center for Educational Leadership, University of Washington. (2014). *Instructional leadership inquiry cycle tool*. Retrieved from https://k-12leadership.org/tools/instructional-leadership-inquiry-cycle-tool/

Costa, A. L., & Garmston, R. J. (2002). *Cognitive coaching: A foundation for renaissance schools*. Norwood, MA: Christopher-Gordon.

Covey, S. (1989). *Seven habits of highly effective people*. New York, NY: Simon & Schuster.

Danielson, C. (1996). *Enhancing professional practice: A framework for teaching*. Alexandria, VA: Association for Supervision and Curriculum Development.

Darling-Hammond, L., Wechsler, M.E., Levin, S., Leung-Gagné, M., & Tozer, S. (2022). *Developing effective principals: What kind of learning matters?* [Report]. Learning Policy Institute. https://doi.org/10.54300/641.201

Echeverría, R. O. (1990). Assertions and assessments. In *Mastering the art of professional coaching* (Vol. §2, pp. 1–11). San Francisco, CA: The Newfield Group.

Echeverría, R. O., & Olalla, J. (1992). The art of ontological coaching. In *Mastering the art of ontological coaching* (Vol. §12, pp. 1–21). San Francisco, CA: The Newfield Group.

Efran, J., & Lukens, M. D. (May–June 1985). The world according to Humberto Maturana. *Family Therapy Networker*, 23–43.

Ekman, P. (2003). *Emotions revealed*. New York, NY: Holt.

Farkas, S., Johnson, J., Duffett, A., & Foleno, T. (with Foley, P). (2001). *Trying to stay ahead of the game: Superintendents and principals talk about school leadership*. New York, NY: Public Agenda.

Feiman-Nemser, S., & Remillard, J. (1995). *Perspectives on learning to teach*. East Lansing, MI: Michigan State University, National Center for Research on Teacher Learning.

Fong, P. (January 27, 2021). *Now is the time for teachers to use data-based inquiry cycles*. Retrieved from https://www.wested.org/wested-insights/rel-west-data-based-inquiry-cycles/

Fullan, M. (1993). *Change forces*. London: Falmer.

Fullan, M. (1997). *What's worth fighting for in the principalship?* New York, NY: Teachers College Press.

Gilley, J. W., & Broughton, N. W. (1996). *Stop managing, start coaching! How performance coaching can enhance commitment and improve productivity.* New York, NY: McGraw-Hill.

Goff, P., Guthrie, E., Goldring, E., & Bickman, L. (2014). Changing principals' leadership through feedback and coaching. *Journal of Educational Administration, 52*(5), 682–704. doi: 10.1108/JEA-10-2013-0113

Goleman, D. (1998). *Working with emotional intelligence.* New York, NY: Bantam Books.

Goleman, D., Boyatzis, R., & McKee, A. (2002). *Primal leadership: Realizing the power of emotional intelligence.* Boston, MA: Harvard Business School Press.

Grissom, J., Egalite, A., & Lindsay, C. (2021). *How principals affect students and schools: A systematic synthesis of two decades of research.* New York, NY: The Wallace Foundation. Retrieved from http://www.wallacefoundation.org/principalsynthesis

Grissom, J., & Harrington, J. R. (2010). Investing in administrator efficacy: An examination of professional development as a tool for enhancing principal effectiveness. *American Journal of Education, 116*(4), 583–612.

Hallinger, P., & Murphy, J. F. (2013). Running on empty? Finding the time and capacity to lead learning. *NASSP Bulletin, 97*(1), 5–21.

Hargrove, R. (1995). *Masterful coaching: Extraordinary results by impacting people and the way they think and work together.* San Francisco, CA: Jossey-Bass.

Helm, C. (2010). Leadership dispositions: What are they and are they essential to good leadership. *Academic Leadership: The Online Journal, 8*(1), 21.

Hobson, A. (2003). *Mentoring and coaching for new leaders.* Nottingham: National College for School Leadership.

Huff, J., Preston, C., & Goldring, E. (2013). Implementation of a coaching program for school principals: Evaluating coaches' strategies and the results. *Educational Management Administration & Leadership, 41*(4), 504–526.

Hatch, T. (2002). When improvement programs collide. *Phi Delta Kappan, 83*(8), 626–639.

Isaacson, N., & Bamburg, J. (November 1992). Can schools become better learning organizations? *Educational Leadership,* 42–44.

Jackson, P. (1995). *Sacred hoops.* New York, NY: Hyperion.

Kouzes, J. P., & Posner, B. (1987). *The leadership challenge.* San Francisco, CA: Jossey-Bass.

Leadership Academy. (2020). *Equity leadership dispositions.* Retrieved from https://www.nycleadershipacademy.org/wp-content/uploads/2020/04/Equity-Leadership-Dispositions.pdf

Lindsey, R., Robins, K., & Terrell, R. (1999). *Cultural proficiency: A manual for school leaders.* Thousand Oaks, CA: Corwin.

Loewenstein, G. (1994). The psychology of curiosity: A review and reinterpretation. *Psychological Bulletin, 116*(1), 75–98.

McLagan, P., & Krembs, P. (1995). *On the level: Performance communication that works.* San Francisco, CA: Berret-Koehler.

Mehrabian, A. (1972). *Nonverbal communication.* Chicago, IL: Aldine-Atherton.

National Policy Board for Educational Administration. (2015). *Professional standards for educational leaders 2015.* Reston, VA: Author.

Neufeld, B., & Roper, D. (2003). *Coaching: A strategy for developing instructional capacity.* Providence, RI: Annenberg Institute.

Patrick, S. K., Rogers, L. K., Goldring, E., Neumerski, C. M., & Robinson, V. (2021). Opening the black box of leadership coaching: An examination of coaching behaviors. *Journal of Educational Administration, 59*(5), 549–563.

Perkins, D. (1995). *Outsmarting I.Q.: The emerging science of learnable intelligence.* New York, NY: The Free Press.

Rath, T. (2007). *StrengthsFinder 2.0.* New York, NY: Gallup Press.

Reiss, K. (2006). *Leadership coaching for educators: Bringing out the best in administrators.* Thousand Oaks, CA: Corwin.

Robinson, V. M. (2007). *School leadership and student outcomes: Identifying what works and why.* Melbourne, VI: Australian Council for Educational Leaders.

Searle, J. R. (1969). *Speech acts.* Cambridge, MA: Cambridge University Press.

Senge, P. M. (1990). *The fifth discipline.* New York, NY: Doubleday.

Speck, M., & Knipe, C. (2001). *Why can't we get it right? Professional development in our schools.* Thousand Oaks, CA: Corwin.

Sullivan, S., & Glantz, J. (2013). *Supervision that improves teaching and learning: Strategies and techniques* (4th ed.). Thousand Oaks, CA: Corwin.

Taylor, R., & Wasicsko, M. (November 4, 2000). The dispositions to teach [Conference presentation]. *Southern region association of teacher educators conference.* Lexington, KY.

Note: The authors suggest to the reader that the following document, while not directly cited in this book, is an important source of information about school leaders: *The Principal, Keystone of a High Achieving School: Attracting and Keeping the Leaders We Need.* (2000). Arlington, VA: published jointly by the National Association of Elementary School Principals and the National Association of Secondary School Principals.

Index

A SAGE Publishing Company

Helping educators make the greatest impact

CORWIN HAS ONE MISSION: to enhance education through intentional professional learning.

We build long-term relationships with our authors, educators, clients, and associations who partner with us to develop and continuously improve the best evidence-based practices that establish and support lifelong learning.

We're Here TO HELP

We are committed to helping you build a coaching-based culture in your organization, a culture that will both support and grow your people in the interest of equitable student success. We may be available to provide

- **Dynamic, highly interactive and customized workshops on Blended Coaching and Coaching-Based Supervision**

- **Training and organizational consultation for school leaders in a variety of roles, building a coaching-based culture and systems in your organization**

- **Consultation and training regarding policy and processes related to supervision, leadership development, and principal pipelines**

For more information, contact

Gary Bloom at
gsbloom@gmail.com

Jackie Owens Wilson at
Drjowilson143@gmail.com

CORWIN